Beowulf: A Pagan Hero

BEOWULF: A PAGAN HERO

A MODERN POETIC TRANSLATION

JULIE BOYDEN

Algora Publishing
New York

Library of Congress Cataloging-in-Publication Data —

Sobchack, Julie Boyden, 1940- author.
  Beowulf, a Pagan Hero: a Modern Poetic Translation / Julie Boyden Sobchack.
    pages cm
    ISBN 978-1-62894-069-5 (soft cover: alk. paper) — ISBN 978-1-62894-
070-1 (hard cover: alk. paper) — ISBN 978-1-62894-071-8 (ebook) 1. Beowulf--
Adaptations. I. Title.
    PS3619.O3736B46 2014
    811'.6--dc23
                              2014001290

Cover photo: Ceremonial helmet recovered from Anglo-Saxon ship burial site
at Sutton Hoo.

Printed in the United States

Acknowledgements

Though it is impossible to name each and every person who helped me get this book out of my head and into print, the following list will have to suffice; if I have overlooked anyone, it is an egregious oversight on my part and you have my most sincere apologies. That said, I am deeply indebted to the following for their love, their help, and their support:

My parents and my grandmother, who taught me to read at a young age, and gave me a love of reading..

My teachers, especially the ones who first uttered the name and deeds of "Beowulf," in Old English.

My husband, children, family, and friends who put up with my incessant reading of and talking about all things Anglo Saxon.

My tutor, who chose *Beowulf* as the epitome of primers for teaching me the Old English language.

J.R.R. Tolkien, who brought *Beowulf* to life in *The Hobbit*, and who ignited my desire to learn the stories behind his brilliant representation of Anglo Saxon "horse lords" in *The Lord of the Rings*.

All the scholars, authors and poets from Grímur Jónsson Thorkelin to Seamus Heaney who made excellent, exacting, exciting, and elegant translations of *Beowulf* for me to immerse myself in.

And finally:

The unnamed poet who wrote out the story that was already ages old before he put quill to parchment and left that remarkable legacy to the world.

For Tom, because he read every word. Twice.

TABLE OF CONTENTS

A Note on Pronunciation

In Old English (Anglo Saxon), every letter is pronounced, including "e" at the end of words. The letters ð and þ are pronounced like the modern "th"; g before e or i is given a "yuh" sound and ic is "itch"; "ea" is a one-syllable "ay-ah", as is "eo" ("ay-oh") and is said quickly. The letter "c" represents "k" except when it comes before e or i in "ceap" (goods), "cild" (child), and "cirice" (church), and names ending in "ic" when it sounds like the modern "ch" sound. The letter "g" may have a hard sound when it follows "c", as in "Ecgtheow", so it sounds like "edge." When a "y" appears in a name or word ("cyning" or "Hæthcyn"), it has a slight "oo" sound, somewhat less than the double-o in "foot." In the body of a word, "f" is pronounced like "v".

When reading *Beowulf*, it helps to know how to pronounce the characters' names. The accent always falls on the first syllable. When a name starts with "Sc" it is pronounced like "sh," as in "Scyld Scefing;" "e" is pronounced as an independent vowel, so "Beowulf" sounds like "bay-oh-wolf. "Heorot" is "Hay-oh-roht," and "Geats" are "Gay-ahts." The letter "H" at the beginning of a name is aspirated (strongly breathed). "Ch" sounds like the "ch" in "Bach" or "loch." The names beginning with "Ea" or "Eo" should be pronounced somewhat like the sounds in "yeah" or "yeoman."

Aelfhere	alf-hair-uh
Aeschere	ash-hair-uh
Beanstan	bayan-stan
Daeghrefn	day-hreven
Eadgils	ayad-gils (hard **g**)
Eanmund	ayan-mund
Earnaness	air-nuh-ness
Ecgtheow	edge-thayow
Eofor	ayo-vor
Freawaru	fraya-wah-roo
Geat	gay-at
Geatas	gayat-as
Hæthcyn	hath-kin
Healfdene	hayelf-day-nuh (pronounce the l)
Heardred	hair-dred
Heorogar	hair-oh-gar
Heorot	hay-oh-roht
Herebeald	hair-uh-bayald
Heremod	hair-uh-mode
Hildeburh	hil-duh-burch (as in **loch**)
Hnaef	naff
Hoc	hoke
Hreosnabeorh	hrayos-nuh-bairch
Hrothgar	hroth-gar
Hronesnes	hron-us-ness
Hygelac	hee-yuh-lahk
Nægling	nail-ing
Ohthere	ocht-hair-uh
Ongentheow	on-gen-thayo (hard **g**)
Scefing	shay-ving
scop	shope

Scyld	shild
Wealhtheow	wayelch-thayo
Weohstan	wayoch-stan
Wiglaf	wee-lahf

Reading *The Hobbit* and *The Lord of the Rings* introduced me to J.R.R. Tolkien in the early 1960s. I understood his Elvish languages came from his own fertile brain, but it was the way he used English in his prose and his poetry that awoke something in my own mind. There was a deep and inexplicable sense of familiarity in the words and phrasing that drew me in. More research and reading about Tolkien led me to the knowledge of his mastery of Old English, the language of the Anglo Saxons. His prose sings with the alliterative sounds of that language, while his choice of words evokes a world so far behind us it is now almost beyond recall, a vast history full of mist and shadow. Years later, when I returned to school, glimmers of that long-ago world reappeared as I listened, spell-bound, to my English Lit professor recite the opening lines of *Beowulf* in its original language, igniting an unquenchable desire to learn Anglo Saxon. My translation of *Beowulf*'s ageless poetry is the years-long culmination of that desire.

Beowulf is an oral story infinitely older than the single surviving copy on display under glass in the British Library. It began centuries ago as a vibrant and entertaining tale told around communal fires to remind listeners of the glory of their fabled past and the strength of their lineage. For a meal and a warm place to spend the night, a wandering *scop*, or storyteller, enthralled eager audiences with the tale of Beowulf, a legendary hero and Monster Slayer. These listeners belonged to a pagan warrior society that trusted in the rule of Fate and the virtue of keeping sworn oaths. Their heroes were men who lived lives of loyalty, honor, bravery, devotion to duty, generosity, and swift, sure vengeance. Beowulf, in the poem, embodied all these desired qualities. In the poem, he becomes super-heroic, relying on an incredible gift (the strength of thirty men in the grip of one hand) to quell his enemies or swim home across a wide sea carrying numerous coats of mail from his fallen companions. His poem tells us he slew fearsome monsters, Grendel and his mother, not only to honor an unpaid debt owed by his dead father to a Danish king, but also to gain fame and personal glory for himself and for his own lord and ring-giver. Beowulf was a man once ridiculed in his youth by his own people for laziness and day-dreaming, an image he put to rest forever by sailing home from his monster-slaying in a ship laden with a hoard of gold and treasure, opulent, visible thanks given to him by a grateful Danish ruler. Eventually, some years after the death of his uncle Hygelac, Beowulf became the revered and respected king of his people and ruled them generously and well for fifty years in peace and prosperity. The poem ends with Beowulf as an old man at the end of his reign, and tells us he faced and fought a hoard-guarding dragon to the death of them both.

This heroic story took its place among the sagas and wonder-tales of the Scandinavian North, and after many generations of oral recitation, it made its way to England with Nordic tribes from Denmark and Jutland plundering the Isles. The poem was eventually written down by an English poet, but there's little chance of finding an "original" piece of that poet's work. Whether or not he was a Christian no one knows, but he seemed very knowledgeable about his nation's pagan past and equally well-versed in its growing faith in Christianity. But he, or someone like him, wrote out the ancient story of Beowulf. No one can say when *Beowulf* was told for the first time. No one can say when it was first written down, though the copy in the museum dates to around AD 1000. But was it the first? The fragile, yellowing manuscript in the British Library is a copy of a copy, and as it sits now, bears the handwriting and translation syntax of two separate people. Did the original poet interject his Christian beliefs into the story of a pagan warrior society? Or did the monks who made copies of that nebulous poet's work interject the Christianity on their own? However it came about, if not for the literate and dutiful Christian monks who made copies of all the known writings of their day, perhaps there would have been no traces of what the Beowulf-poet wrote. And the literary world would have been poorer for it.

The North-men have a long and storied past; some of the stories are grim, even gruesome, but most are well-worth the telling or the reading. These are tales born in the long dark of Northern winters, entertaining tales of gods with human foibles; explanations of how the Norse gods created the world and why; tales of fantastically strong men; women of pale beauty given in marriage as peace-pledges to neighboring kings; dragons and dwarves; giants, elves, and orcs; shape-changers and were-creatures. They are stories of the value of a man's word and his duty to seek and win the highest prize of all—eternal fame and glory for bravery in the brutal life-or-death clashes in the shield-wall of war. Oath-keepers and those who gained glory through great deeds were valued as the best of men, designated worthy of gifts from the lords of their nations and chieftains of their tribes. Deceit brought dishonor, not only to the deceitful, but to his clan and nation. Those tales sparked exploration, trading and colonization, but they also led to raiding, both on land and sea. Heroic stories from the fogs and mists of the Nordic cold were inspiration for songs, fairytales, operas, and sweeping epic novels.

So, why another translation of *Beowulf*? I wanted to tell the story of Beowulf as it might have been told in its beginnings, a story uninflected by any softening influences of language or Christianity. The best way to accomplish that, I reasoned, was to learn the language of the poem. Old English, or Anglo Saxon, is a language of burly power, yet startling at times in the alliterative beauty of its words and sounds, a language spoken by heroes and warriors who have long since passed into the realm of history. As I learned more about the language and the world of Beowulf, my desire also grew to tell the story as it must have originated around embered fires, in pagan minds and voices, with all the Dark Age ethos and ideals intact. I began by taking away the Christian insertions, even the poetic ones. Doing that revealed the absolute bedrock of a culture and people who struggled with inhospitable lands, struck out on unknown seas, and discovered new worlds. Taking away the Christian overtones exposed the hard core of the Norse belief in the rule of Fate, an unpersuadable force that controlled a man's unknowable but ultimate destiny. I discovered that by removing the Christian references, it brought me closer to the language that formed the poem as it was first written, its forceful and rhythmic sounds telling a stillpopular story of courage, fearlessness, and honor.

In my translation, I have let the words and their poetry speak for themselves, seeking for the feelings of the poet who wrote it into history. I concentrated more on the words that poet wrote and less on trying to make my own words fit the Anglo Saxon alliterative rhythm. Nevertheless, Modern English alliteration seemed to fall naturally into place, but it didn't maintain the fourcount stressed rhythm of a line, followed by a caesura, and then a lesser stressed fourcount line. It was the *skalds* reciting the poem who gave it the rhythmic, alliterative form we are familiar with, but the pages of the manuscript I have seen in the British Library do not look like that. The words follow one another in a nearly endless succession, seemingly without punctuation, very few capital letters, or rests between phrases. My biggest problem came from trying to fit the syntax of those early words into a more understandable form for modern readers. For the most part, I believe I have succeeded.

By retaining as much as possible of the feel and sense of the original Old English/Anglo Saxon language, and relying as little as possible on terms and words that began to filter into the English language after 1066, I hoped to bring readers not only closer to the culture of Beowulf's society, but also to the poetry in the sounds of that language. *Beowulf* was meant to be recited. Its language demands it. And *Beowulf* still has much to teach us. *Beowulf* is a journey story, a journey full of peril and danger and ultimate triumph, a victory at great cost. It is a journey along a glory-dappled road from youthful strength to thoughtful old age. It is a journey into the most perilous territory of all—the human psyche—to find wisdom and redemption and immortal glory.

BEOWULF: INTRODUCTION TO A PAGAN HERO

Beowulf, the iconic Anglo Saxon (Old English) poem, is the oldest piece of writing in the English literary canon which still, to this present day, appears regularly as assigned reading in British Literature classes. The only existing copy is over a thousand years old, and rests under protective glass in the British Library in London, in England. The writing of it is credited to an unnamed English poet. But in spite of all these English connections, *Beowulf* deals neither with native Englishmen nor events that took place on English soil. Instead, it is the written account of an oral story concerning two Scandinavian tribes—the Danes from Zealand, and the Geats from southern Sweden. The names of kings and rulers in the poem are recorded in those nations' genealogies from the Fourth Century, and certain events in the poem are described in ancient histories of both Denmark and Sweden. When the Nordic tribes began their invasions of the British Isles, not only did they bring their history and their language—they also brought with them the story of Beowulf.

The recorded dates of those invasions and subsequent set-tlements in Britain suggest *Beowulf* was an immeasurably old story before that unnamed poet transcribed it sometime between AD 700 and 1000. During those years, England's long-established pagan traditions had all but disappeared, giving Christianity the upper hand. But no one can say whether or not the poet who put the ancient story into written form was a Christian, for without knowing his name or anything else about him, there is no sure way to affirm his beliefs. It is also equally difficult to say how clearly *Beowulf* represents the Christianity of that early time, as the poem never mentions Christ or his sacrifice, two founding principles of that religion. There are, however, numerous Old Testament references: God is said to be the creator of all, with his will mirroring Fate (*wyrd*). We are told the monster, Grendel, is a descendant of Cain, the bible's first murderer. And some read Hrothgar's lengthy advice to Beowulf (lines 1700 to 1783) as a warning to maintain Christian virtues in order to succeed as a revered ruler. Yet the invocation of Christian values is not what has given this poem its remarkable longevity. For instance, that speech of Hrothgar's to Beowulf can easily be read as words of advice from an old experienced ruler to a younger future king, directed more toward making him a good leader of men than a good Christian. It is therefore safe to say the story of *Beowulf* that came to early Britain with the invaders from across the North Sea was not of Christian origin.

The heroic way of life informing this poem is clearly pre-Christian, full of pagan burial rites and customs, and an embodiment of the rules that bound the warrior society together. Those same ideals and practices are mirrored in the concept of *virtus* in Latin, and *areté*, in Greek, traits epitomized in the lives and actions of the heroes of *The Odyssey* and *The Iliad*, which have survived these past ages without Christianity adding anything to them. So, in order for readers to fully experience *Beowulf* as it was first told, it was necessary to divest it of all Christian references and take it back to its earlier beginnings, which I have done. My aim was to stay as close as possible to the original Anglo Saxon language and linguistics of the poem, and in my translation to limit the use of words or phrases that came into the English language after AD 1066. Stripping away the Christian allusions reveals the warrior culture as it truly existed in those times.

The society that produced the story of *Beowulf* might, wrongly, be considered by many as nasty, or brutish, even primitive; but that long-lost society exemplified a firm trust in Fate (*wyrd*), a strict code of honor, loyalty, and oath-keeping, the importance of doing one's duty, and the bone-deep necessity of winning eternal fame. *Beowulf* emphasizes gaining glory for both a man and the king he served through bravery in battle. This poem sings with the joy and supremacy of defeating enemies through a war-band's strength and prowess, and exalts the almost holy reverence for valor in the shield-wall of war. The power and renown sought and celebrated by rulers and warriors in the world of *Beowulf* stands well apart from any connection with Christian values. To this society, fame on this earth, not a heavenly resurrection, was the highest reward.

That long-gone society also produced craftsmen proficient in metal-working, gold-smithing, and jewelry making. Relics and artifacts from that period are replete with intricately worked clasps on purses, jeweled sword-hilts, pins and brooches of amazing artistry, closely linked chain mail and what the *Beowulf* poet describes as "steep helmets," head-protectors so ornately carved and highly polished it showed friend and foe alike that here was a warrior to be reckoned with. Weavers wove richly dyed wool into cloaks, some trimmed with fur, cinched up with deeply embossed belts of woven leather clasped with elaborate buckles. Not only the lords of the various tribes and clans, but also the lords of war in that society must have made an impressive sight.

At the time of the historical events in the poem, Christianity had not yet succeeded in purging Northern lands of their older pagan traditions, which still evoked powerful responses from men's hearts. This warrior society contained no devil to punish those who err and no Christ to bless those who live a moral life, and without those factors, the narrative of the poem becomes clearer; one can see and understand the faith warriors placed in their own honorable actions and the earthly rewards they earned by following their society's rules. The afterlife they sought could only be gained by those who died bravely, weapon in hand, chosen by Odin as one of his beloved thanes and given a seat at his roisterous mead-bench in Valhalla. As Beowulf says:

"Each of us must abide [accept] the end of our life in this world and gain glory before death." (XXI-1383)

The promise of God-given rewards for living a life built on Christian principles plays no part in the lives of the warriors in *Beowulf*, and certainly could not have been part of the poem's original telling. In that far distant age, poets wove their words at the time of the telling; the story, in the hands of an expert poet, or *scop*, was valued not only for what it told the audience but for how it entertained them. Surely the *Beowulf* poet knew that. It is easy to imagine that as Christianity grew in strength, and the audience grew more aware of it, those tenets began to creep into the telling of *Beowulf*, too. Insertions concerning the new religion appear in other manuscripts copied by Christian monks hard at work in scriptoriums and monasteries, reproducing any and all written works of their time, eventually including the *Beowulf* manuscript. The intent of any insertions, written or oral, was surely to show the pagan audience whatever similarities might exist between their old gods and the new god of Christianity. The monks also translated many books of the bible into Old English; *Exodus*, for one, was turned into a story of a war-band (soldiers from the Tribes of Israel) serving wise and heroic leaders (Moses and Aaron) to vanquish their enemies (Pharaoh's troops). The conversion of pagans would be more easily accomplished if the monks could promote Christianity by interlacing it with the heroic exploits of persons from their own ancestry (i.e., *Beowulf*).

One of the Christian additions to the poem describes Grendel as a descendant of Cain, the Old Testament's first murderer. But Grendel is truly a Northern monster, a creature with no lineage given except for monster-kind:

"He was a wretched creature

kin to all un-things,

ogres and elves and giants

who fought a long time against the race of men." (103 - 104)

The people who lived in the moors and the fastness of the fens surrounding Hrothgar's mead-hall, Heorot, give this description of Grendel and his monstrous mother:

". . . two demon-spirits

haunting the moors and marking exile paths.

As clearly as they could see,

one of them was of a woman's likeness.

The other was man-shaped,

but wretched, larger than other men.

From ancient times

the earth-dwellers named him Grendel.

They did not know his father,

or whether he had been born of hidden spirits." (1345 - 1353)

Ogres, elves, giants, and demons inhabit the vast terrain of other Norse stories, myths, and legends, where Cain's name never appears as part of their lineage. Grendel is a shadow-stalker rushing out of the dark to savage Heorot's mead-hall because he is excluded from its world of joy, revelry, and boisterous camaraderie. He invades Heorot because his own world is joyless, lawless, and dark. Some interpret Grendel and his kind allegorically, identifying them as inner demons that harry mankind, while the insertions made by Christian monks in *Beowulf* tell us to believe these monsters are examples of tests from a God who must be implored for strength to fight them. But there is another way to look at this monster—the description of Grendel and his rage against the Danes fits the description of a more sinister kind of warrior in this society: the *berserker*. In the old stories, it is said that *berserkers* "shape-change" into bears or wolves; that they are warriors whose very visage alters when faced with battle; it is said they become "swollen with anger," or "purple with rage;" that they hew and hack at all before them without regard to friend or foe; and that they seem impervious to weapons wielded against them. Warriors of this ilk had no real place in the society around them because of their excessive violence. But the presence of these creatures and their behaviors in the tales and sagas from the North served to emphasize the pagan warrior society's steadfast belief that all things in their world, even monstrous things, could be mastered by a man's own strength and willing heart. A man's prowess would gain him much sought-after and highly prized fame and glory on this earth, regardless of whether or not he was taken up into Odin's realm.

Odin's mead-benches were best represented on this earth by Hrothgar's fabulous mead-hall, Heorot, described by the poet as having timbers and door lintels gilded, gold adorned, walls hung with brightly colored tapestries, and deeply carved mead-benches and tables for the drinkers' revels. It was a place for the warriors to meet at night, to drink mead and beer, to hear the songs and tales that made their lineage come alive for them, to swear their binding oaths to their lord and to each other. Gold was shared out to the warriors from the throne, called "the gift seat", by their generous lord and ring-giver. Generosity was a highly prized virtue, with the best of men being the most generous. Music and laughter must have rung loudly through the night, until the benches were cleared, bolsters and bedding were spread across the floors, and men went to their rest.

The most important human relationship in the warrior society that gave us *Beowulf* existed not between a man and any named or un-named god, but between a thane and his earthly lord, a unity based not on subordination of one man's will to another's, but on mutual trust and respect. By swearing allegiance and loyalty to a wise and generous lord, the warrior became a faithful "shoulder-companion," an "oath-man" who could take great pride in defending that lord by fighting in his shield-wall. (In a timeline of early Swedish history, a warrior named Beowulf is listed as participating in a raid on the Franks under the leadership of his lord and uncle, Hygelac, king of the Geats in AD 520.) In return, a worthy king was expected to take good, even familial, care of his valiant thanes, to give generous gifts for their every brave deed. Worthy kings like Hygelac, Hrothgar, and Beowulf were praised with titles such as "ring-giver," "protector of the people," "treasure-giver," "warriors' shield." This relationship between thane and lord was not based on material gain but on trust, on the duty of honoring sworn oaths, and on total reliance on each other in the shared peril of battle. Treasure seized from his enemies by a good king was divided among his hand-picked thanes as a sign of more than mere wealth; this was easily-seen evidence that the men he had chosen for his war-band were loyally united with one another in true brotherhood (the Latin term for this kind of comradeship is *comitatus*; while the Old English is *drengr*, or *druhtin*). Beowulf makes this clear as he readies himself and his thanes to follow after Grendel's murderous mother. He tells Hrothgar:

> ". . . if in your service I should yield up my life,
>
> then you would ever be in my father's place.
>
> If this battle takes me, protect my young kin-thanes,
>
> my hand-chosen war band.
>
> Beloved Hrothgar, all the treasures you gave me
>
> send on to Hygelac, son of Hrethel.
>
> When he stares on the gold-gleaming treasure,
>
> may that Geats' lord
>
> see that I found a good king, a generous ring-giver,
>
> and enjoyed life while I served him."
>
> (1481-1489)

Along with the strength of unity among the warriors, the familial bonds between kinsmen also formed a substantial part of the social relationships throughout the entire community, adding another emotional layer to the Old English world of *Beowulf*. If a man's kinsman was slain, that man was bound by his duty to society either to kill the slayer or exact *wergild* (man-price) from him, definitely not Christian behavior. Each level of that society, from lord to slave, had been given a monetary value, and a killing, even an accidental one, required the killer to make swift payment to the dead man's kin or suffer their vengeance. The payment itself carried less importance than providing unarguable evidence the killer had honored his commitment to the social contract at that time. Those who could not exact *wergild* or vengeance could never find comfort or satisfaction, having no adequate way to give or take recompense for their kinsman's death. The consequence of having to make such a harrowing choice is made clear in one of the most poignant episodes in the poem—the story of King Hrethel after one of his sons, Hæthcyn, accidentally kills his own brother, Herebeald:

"Each morning the father

remembers his son's death-day

with an aching heart.

In his son's empty house

he sees a wasted wine-hall,

a wind-swept refuge bereft of joy,

the riders and heroes asleep in graves.

There is no sound of harp or laughter

on the benches as there once was.

So that grieving father seeks his bed,

singing sorrow-dirges for himself

and for his dead son.

In his grief, Hrethel finds the fields and dwelling places

boundless, too empty.

The Wederas' leader suffers sorrow-surges for Herebeald,

but for Hæthcyn the kin-slayer,

he feels neither hate nor love.

So Hrethel gave up men's joys

and put himself into Fate's keeping."

(2453-2461)

In accordance with the laws of kinship, Hrethel was forbidden to either take compensation from his own son or to kill him, yet that same law required him to do one or the other in order to avenge the dead. That terrible dichotomy proved too much for Hrethel, and the poem tells us he left this life in order to quell his anguish. If the *Beowulf* poet had been a Christian, it is hard to believe he would have left this aspect of warrior society intact in the poem, for there is no preaching of forgiveness here, no admonition to "turn the other cheek," and certainly no condoning of what could be read or understood as a grief-driven suicide.

This endless (and un-Christian) requirement to take vengeance encouraged the practice of marrying royal daughters and sisters to kings or princes of rival tribes, a grand but futile gesture which rarely provided a permanent end to tribal conflicts. Hrothgar gave his daughter, Freawaru, in marriage to Ingeld, king of the Heatho-Bards, because Hrothgar's warriors had killed Ingeld's father. Later, in a conversation with his uncle Hygelac, Beowulf predicts that sooner or later those same Heatho-Bards' need for vengeance would spill over and there would be more bloodshed. "[V]ery seldom does the deadly spear lie idle for long, though the bride is good." (2030 - 2031) The Danish princess Hildeburh, married as a peace-pledge to Finn of the Jutes, saw both her son and her brother killed while fighting on opposite sides in a battle waged in the fields outside her own mead-hall. Later, Finn, her husband, was slain by her own people in revenge for her brother's death. The imminence and inevitability of violent change and swift death pervade *Beowulf*, an immense, tangled knot of reprisals and counter-reprisals impossible to alter. Fate and revenge work hand in hand to prove there is no escaping a man's destiny. At the same time, it is this relentless repetition of vengeance and retribution that makes the biggest and most potent impression on readers and shows us why many scholars have declared *Beowulf* more elegy than poem.

Beowulf's monster-slaying comes about not because of tribal feuds, but because of an evil more complex than any in the poem, a force operating completely outside the rule of *wyrd*, beyond the scope of men or their gods, far outside their society. The three foes—Grendel, his mother, the dragon—threaten the security of the lands they inhabit as surely as human enemies would, but their realm is totally outside the social order: these beings have no one to avenge their deaths or to seek *wergild* from their slayer. (When Grendel's mother appears in Heorot to avenge her son's death, it seems to surprise both Beowulf and the Danes). Because these fiends are not part of the normal order of things, they demand of their slayer something greater than normal warfare. So if the king and his warriors wish to stay true to their society's code, they are bound by duty to utterly destroy them, relying on their faith in Fate and their own warrior-strength to eradicate these demonic foes. But Hrothgar is old and he and his war-band have aged away from their former sense of adventure or need to prove their prowess. Excellent though Hrothgar has been as a king, he has lost a quality (*heardhicgende* – a brave hardness of mind) that the aged Beowulf will readily call upon within himself when he must fight the dragon that threatens his own people. Hrothgar is never criticized for this lack because it is understood it was not his fate to develop his full potential to the extent *wyrd* would permit. That deed is for Beowulf to accomplish. In taking on Grendel and later Grendel's mother, Beowulf is testing his life-long reliance on unknowable destiny, knowing full well that at any time his luck may fail and it will then become his fate to suffer death. Yet, never once does he call upon either a Christian god or Odin with a plea for safety or success; whether he lives or dies, he will have done all a man can do to develop his own character to the fullest heroic ideal.

Beowulf's conscious testing of Fate spurs the boasting we hear from him throughout the poem, another trait never encouraged in the Christian faith, but always a part of the warrior world. Odysseus, Aeneas, Ajax, all the heroes of the Greek legends, are epic boasters; it is a trait encouraged in great warriors. Through his boasting, Beowulf shows that not only has he chosen the heroic way of life, but that his nearly superhuman exploits have exhibited his constant reaffirmation of that choice. He puts himself not into the care of a Christian God, but squarely into the hands of Fate (*wyrd*) and his own legendary strength to seek his high destiny. By invoking his past deeds as a sign of his intentions toward committing further courage-deeds, his boasts become vows, putting him irrevocably in the place of no withdrawal, for no Northern, pagan, hero would ever consider breaking an oath he'd made in love and service to his people or his lord. Courage, not service to God, is the instrument by which Beowulf actualizes himself. "Fate often saves an undoomed man when his heart is good," he says in the account of his swimming match with Breca near the beginning of the poem. (572) What he means is that if Fate hasn't doomed him in advance, his courage can convince Fate not to doom him now. This complex statement is what makes it difficult to understand the insertion of the will of God (and thus, all the other Christian references) into the poem in place of the power of Fate (*wyrd*) that Beowulf's life explores. He will use his great strength in the most courageous exploits, going alone, even unarmed, against every threat, because it is his duty to do so. He has given his word, made an oath, to do so. Doom will ultimately claim him, of course, but not before he has fulfilled the pagan ideals of a heroic life and an honorable death:

"Then around the barrow

rode twelve mounted battle-brave men,

sons of nobles,

who wished to mourn their king,

lament their sorrow.

It is fitting that men

honor their friend-lord

with words and heart-love

when he must give up

his bone-house.

They made a song which men still sing about Beowulf,

and in this manner did the Geats' people,

Beowulf's hearth-companions,

lament their lord's fall:

They praised his courage-deeds and his heroic acts,

exalted his excellence.

They said of him that of all the world-kings

he was the mildest and most gentle,

to his nation the kindest,

and a man most glad to win glory." (3170-3182)

PRINCIPAL CHARACTERS IN BEOWULF

Beowulf
Ecgtheow
Grendel
Hrothgar
Hygelac
Scyld Scefing
Unferth
Wealhtheow
Wiglaf

Beowulf, the hero of this poem, is a name found in early historical genealogies of the Swedish Geats in the Third and Fourth Centuries. Like Arthur in Britain, heroic deeds accrued to Beowulf's name from other Norse legends (Bödvar Bjarki, the Bear's Sons Tales), giving his feats an air of mythic power. In the eponymous poem, we read that Beowulf had been ridiculed in his youth for being lazy and unproductive; it was said by the men on the mead-benches that there would never be any songs sung of his prowess, and that he would never find the fame and renown so important to warriors of that time. Yet Beowulf's courageous deeds won him more fame and glory than anyone else of his tribe, and his name echoes down the ages to our own time in that iconic poem of his heroic life and exploits.

Ecgtheow, Beowulf's father, renowned for his own mighty deeds, fell on hard times and lacked the where-with-all to pay wergild for the men he cut down with his sword. We read in the poem that Ecgtheow gave his son, Beowulf, to his brother Hrethric, to raise as his own. Hygelac, Hrethric's son, became Beowulf's lord. Some time later, Ecgtheow was saved from ignominy by Hrothgar, who paid wergild for all his debts and became his liege-lord. Before Ecgtheow disappeared from the poem, and from history, he swore an oath that he and his kin would be indebted to Hrothgar until the debt could be repaid. Beowulf's deeds in the Danish kingdom settled that debt.

Grendel, a vile monster, lives outside the bounds of a society filled with the joy of war and revelry in the mead halls, excluding him from the deep brothers-in-arms camaraderie of shield-warriors. The *Beowulf* poet writes that Grendel is a creature with no known lineage. In our present time, we struggle to find terms for a being like Grendel. Criminals of some magnitude are sometimes termed "monsters," a fitting title for people who commit hideous acts against humanity, repellant to our present social mores. But Grendel also fits a theory that he could have been a "berserker," a warrior so consumed by violence and the frenzy of war that he wreaked havoc on everyone in his path, whether "friend" or foe, which would certainly exile him—and anyone like him—from the society of his time.

Hrothgar, an aged Danish king known for his generous gold-giving and virtue, suffers attacks upon his famed mead-hall every night for twelve years at Grendel's hands. At dawn, the monster would retreat to his own lair, leaving behind the blood-soaked wreckage of his terror. The daylight hours bring no comfort to the beleaguered Danes, for in the poem it is hinted that life under Grendel's unceasing attacks has become grim and onerous, with no one in the Danish army willing or able to end Grendel's reign of terror. Hrothgar's sorrow over this horror ran deep in his mind, because in his youth he had been a formidable warrior, a generous ring-giver, a king of wide-reaching fame. When we meet him in the poem, he is described as "hoary with age," captain of a war-band that has seen stronger days. Hrothgar mourns his youth and strength, telling and re-telling feats of his former glory.

Hygelac, Beowulf's uncle, lord and ring-giver, is full of youthful vigor and in the peak of his power. Ecgtheow, married to Hygelac's sister, placed the boy Beowulf in Hygelac's care after he became indebted to Hrothgar; Hygelac's example of a ruler bearing all the worthy traits of wisdom, bravery, and generosity helped Beowulf develop into the mightiest warrior in the Geatish nation. But Hygelac was killed in an ill-advised battle with the Franks (noted in the Swedish histories as about AD 520), leaving his people under the care of Hæthcyn, his youngest son. Some years after that, Beowulf inherits the Geatish kingdom and rules it for fifty years.

Scyld Scefing is the first person we meet in the poem, at his funeral. We read that Scyld, a child, alone in a boat, had been sent to the Danish shores "by unseen hands," and under their care had become a mighty and well-loved warrior who grew into a beloved king in Denmark. His funeral rites are described in the richest terms: uncounted gold and treasure is amassed on Scyld's dead body, which had been placed by the tall mast of his ice-draped funeral ship. The ship is further adorned with shields and battle gear. After a bright gold banner is set on the high mast, the ship is commended to winter's cold waves. It disappears into the icy dark night and into history. The poem also tells us that no man, however wise, knew what shores received that hoard-laden vessel.

Unferth is Hrothgar's "reciter," a man of words and keeper of the nation's songs and stories. A man in that position also served as a "provocateur," stirring up controversy with the aim of glorifying or defaming someone famous. Full of envy and drunken from feasting, he ridicules Beowulf for his boasts about swimming with Breca in their youth and besting him. He warns the Danes that nothing good will come to them if they put Beowulf in charge of killing Grendel. But when Beowulf killed Grendel and hung his arm and shoulder under the eaves of Heorot, Unferth was rendered silent (the poem says "no one was more silent"). Barely noticed in the poet's rendering of Unferth is the chilling fact that at some point in his past he had slain his brothers. He removed some of his personal tarnish by loaning Beowulf his sword, Hrunting, to battle Grendel's hideous mother. After that battle, Beowulf returned the sword to Unferth, saying no words against either the sword or its owner.

Wealhtheow, queen of the Danes, is Hrothgar's wife. Reading the poem, it seems Wealhtheow (of the Wulfing dynasty) was given to Hrothgar as a pledge of peace between that tribe and Hrothgar's Danes. She welcomes Beowulf and his warriors to Heorot as a good queen and peace-weaver should—with mead in golden cups and words of praise and hope. Weahltheow is mother to two sons with Hrothgar—Hrethric and Hrothmund. She reminds the very successful Beowulf that it is her sons who will inherit Denmark from their father, for she fears that Hrothgar "wishing Beowulf for his own" will turn the kingdom over to Beowulf instead. In a bit of irony, Wealhtheow commends her two sons to Hrothulf, Hrothgar's nephew, for safekeeping, but later Hrothulf has them killed and takes the kingdom for himself.

Wiglaf is Beowulf's nephew and youngest warrior. He alone stands with Beowulf, the aging king of his people, when he faces his last and greatest foe, a centuries-old dragon who guards a fabulous ancient hoard in a stone barrow under a sea-cliff. The poem recounts the numerous years the enormous hoard lay buried and gives us a plaintive song sung by the man who put it into the cave beneath the gray stone cliffs, "the last survivor" of a once rich and mighty nation. Wiglaf it is who berates the hand-picked band of men Beowulf chose to accompany him to the dragon's lair, the men who desert him at the first breath of fire and heat from the dragon.

Beowulf

Listen!

We have long heard the sagas of the Spear-Danes

whose princes won power through brave deeds

and gladly gained glory

for their loved lords and ring-givers.

Many times Scyld Scefing shamed his enemies

when he terrified their earls,

wrecked their mead-benches,

and made them his own.

Scyld was young in years

when the Danes found him

floating on the wave-foam,

helpless and alone in a boat

sent to their shores by unseen hands.

He grew mighty in their care

and with his war-band he rode

widely through surrounding lands.

He fared far upon the waterways

until every lord of the whale-road

yielded up gold and bent their knee to him.

That was a good king!

After a time a son was born to him,

Beow, young in the world,

a light in darkness long endured,

a comfort to the Danes

who had lived a long while in cold grief.

Many sang songs of Beow's prowess

and rumor of his fame spread far.

He was Scyld's son, glory of the Danish lands.

His good deeds ensured him many fee gifts

while he grew up in his father's care

so that in his winter years,

strong battle-friends

stood with him in the shield-wall when war came.

At his destined time,

Scyld died in the peak of his power

to fare in fate's keeping.

His shield-thanes

carried him down to the sea-streams,

his wishes made clear to his dearest friends

when he wielded words

in younger days.

Ready on the harbor waves rode a hero's vessel,

its proud neck ringed with ice and eager to sail.

Bent with mind-grief

they brought their prince and beloved ring-giver

to the bosom of the ship and laid him down,

a mighty lord, by the mast.

Many treasures and fortunes

were brought from far-away,

and the keel was arrayed

with battle weapons and war-clothes,

blades and byrnies.

On Scyld's bosom were laid many treasures

for his travels far off across the flood.

I have never heard of a grave-ship more richly adorned!

No less did his own people provide for him

than did those

who first sent out the treasure-child,

sailing alone across the sea.

At the last, high atop the mast over his head,

they set Scyld's gold-woven battle-standard.

The war-banner took the wind like a sea-bird's wings

and the mourners gave the boat to the waves.

No man, not warrior, hero, or sage,

can truthfully say who under heaven received that ship.

After that, Beow the Scylding

ruled the realms a long while

like his departed father,

a loved king and lord of the land.

To him was born high-minded Halfdeane

who gladdened the Scyldings until he gained great age.

During his time he fathered four, gave to the world

Heorogar, Hrothgar, Halga the good,

and Yrse, a fair daughter

who became, as I have heard,

queen and bedmate to Onela the battle-Swede.

To Hrothgar was given war-luck and honor in battle.

His hall-thanes he kept close as kinsmen,

youthful warrior-princes

who became powerful shield-men.

It was then Hrothgar thought to build

a mighty mead-hall

like nothing ever known to any living man.

Within its high walls

he would deal out to young and old

such wealth as Fate allowed.

Carpenters, builders, and weavers

came from all over the middle-earth

to raise the towering walls

and gild them with gold

until that hall stood

taller than any.

It shone over all the lands,

brightly adorned, and beautiful.

He who ruled the world of the Danes

named it Heorot.

Hrothgar, famed king, kept his promises

and from his treasure-seat

he gave out rings and gold gifts,

and banished war's ravens.

Heorot's high crossed gables,

capped with golden beams,

could not know of the anger and hate-flames

that awaited them.

It was still too soon

for swords and shields to clash,

not yet the day

for deadly throne-battles

between a blood-minded son and his bride's father.

Out on the moors, a bold demon

exiled from men and dwelling in darkness,

hated the sounds

of rejoicing and revelry loud in Heorot.

He loathed the harp-sway,

the poet singing of ages long past

when the Allfather and his company of gods

brought forth the world.

They formed the bright fields

and encompassed them with seas.

They shaped the Sun and the Moon in the sky

to shed lustrous light on the land,

softened stony folds with limbs and leaves,

and quickened with life

all creatures who call middle-earth home.

So the Danes lived joyously and happily in Heorot

until that fiend came, a ghastly foe called Grendel.

The ill-famed marsh-walker ruled the moors

and the fastness of the fens.

He was a wretched creature

kin to all un-things, ogres and elves and giants,

who fought a long time against the race of men.

Helmed in darkness,

the shadow-stalker crept toward Heorot

to see how the Ring-Danes

fared after feasting and drinking.

He found the band of hall-thanes sleeping soundly

knowing neither sorrow nor the misery of men.

Fierce and grim, Grendel stepped closer

and pulled thirty thanes from their rest.

Howling his victory and greedy with corpses

he loped toward his dwelling

to devour his loathsome death-feast.

When dawn came,

the shadow-walker's war-skill met their eyes,

and instead of feast-glee,

a mourning song arose;

woe and wailing filled men's throats.

Hrothgar, noble and good from early days,

listened without heart,

full of thane-sorrow,

suffering the demon's death-shadows,

thinking the struggle ahead too long,

the fiend too strong.

The next night the marsh-demon returned with the darkness

and brought more murder to the death-hall.

He did not mourn his deeds.

His mind was firmly fixed on destroying the Danes.

After that

it grew easy to find men

who sought shelter further off,

who slept elsewhere,

finding beds among the bowers

to escape the marsh-harrier's hatred

of the hall-thanes.

He who wished to hide from death

did not bed down in Heorot.

Thus did the monster rule,

one lone ravager against all,

until the darkened mead hall stood bereft of joy,

cold-hearthed, and still.

For a great while, twelve winter-times,

the lord of the Danes endured all troubles,

miseries,

and never-ending sorrows,

until to men and to mens' sons

it became widely known

that death dwelled in Denmark.

Sorrow-songs were sung

of Grendel's strife with the Scyldings.

The hall-fiend, named Hel-feeder,

hungered for nightfall.

A wight with no pity and no remorse,

the foe would not seek peace

with any man in the army of Danes.

He would neither quell his rampage

nor atone with fees.

There was no hope for either a wise man or a hero

to gain wergild from the ruiner's hands.

The dark death-shadow stalked veterans and youths,

he lurked and ambushed,

glided unseen through mist-drenched moors

in the endless night where men would not follow.

The grim deeds of the Hel-fiend grew

as the dreaded lone-walker

worked his wrath on the Danes.

Heorot belonged to the death-dealer;

during long black nights

he wandered the once proud hall

and sat before the Scylding's empty gift-seat,

but Grendel knew

he would never gain war-treasure,

never find favor

from the lord who owned that throne.

Many keen men often took counsel together,

speaking about the best campaign

for bold-hearts to take against such horror.

At times they went to the forest

at the first glimmer of the sun

to offer up their best beasts and ask the gods

to take away the thane-slayer

and give them a way out of this plight.

Hrothgar, wise old hero,

could not turn away the woe,

and he seethed in his spirit.

The strife that had come upon his own people

was harsh, loathsome and lengthy,

and the greatest of all night terrors.

Across the waves,

word of Grendel's war with Hrothgar

came to the land of the Geats,

to the ears of Hygelac's thane,

the strongest of all men,

the bravest of all warriors,

the best man in this time.

He ordered a boat, a strong wave-cleaver

well-built for his ride

over the swan-road,

saying he would seek the Battle-Danes

through the wave-foam.

He would aid their lord and ring-giver

and make strong their hearts.

Though he was dearly loved in his own land

leaders long full of wisdom

urged him on his voyage.

They read signs and omens and looked to the sky,

hoping for the sun.

Hygelac's champion

chose his spearmen carefully

and drew from the Geats

their greatest fighters,

all of them

oath-keepers strong and true.

There were fifteen in all

who marched to the sea-cliffs

to find their ship

and follow their chief to the wave-foam.

There at the headland awaited their boat,

riding the sea-swirls

where the waves met the sand.

They set their war-weapons in the ship,

strong spears and bright helmets,

glinting shields and fire-forged swords,

bright battle gear for brave Geats.

Some men leaped aboard

while others strove in the water

to push the boat into the waves.

The sail took the wind

and the strong-built craft

rejoiced in the sea, bound for Denmark.

The ring-prow flew across wind-blown waves

like a bird for a day and a night,

and when dawn came again

the sea-farers could see the land they sought.

In the rising sun sea-cliffs shone

and wave-wet rocks stood sentinel.

The sea-surge gentled, the sail emptied,

and in the shallows the shore received them.

The war-band of Weather-Geats beached their boat

and lashed it to the land.

Steel-ringed battle-shirts rang and glistened

as the sea-riders leaped ashore

and offered joyous thanks

to the Lords of the Sea

for a safe journey.

From the cliff-tops, the Danish land-warden

watched with keen eyes

and marked in his mind

the gleaming armor borne from their boat,

the war-weapons, spears,

bright shields and broad swords.

He mounted his horse

and rode swiftly down to the shore.

Hrothgar's coast guard shook his spear

and shouted a challenge:

    "Who are you men, armed for battle

     with your burnished war-shirts

    and long spears?

    Who piloted this proud craft to these shores?

    Be warned!

    I have long kept guard against sailors like you.

    I have watched over Denmark

    through long years

    so no ship-band

    might make harbor unfought.

    Never in those years has a ship

    beached so openly.

    Never have shield-bearing thanes

    unsure of welcome

    hoisted no flags,

    or failed to signal with peace-tokens

    their friendship with Danes.

    Nor have I ever challenged

    a worthier shield-man

    than one who stands among you

    stalwart in his war-gear;

    one so weapon-worthy

    is no stranger to battle.

    I hope his wit is equal to his sword-play.

    Tell me quickly who sent you

and where you came from
before you possible pirates
push further into the land of the Danes.
I will advise you horseless sailors
to heed my heartfelt words:
Hasty answers will be strong help in telling me
the land you came from."

Then Beowulf, prince of the Geats,
unlocked his word hoard:
"We are men of the Geats,
lord Hygelac's trusted hearth-companions
and mindful of our manners.
My father, Ecgtheow is his name,
long wandered through the world
and earned his way to Geat-land.
He survived many winters
in wartime and peace
until age finally wearied him.
Songs of his battle-victories
are still sung
by wise men widely through the world.
We have come here today
with best intentions
to seek out your lord Hrothgar,
son of Healfdeane,
victor of the Scyldings.
Be our good guide.
We hold no secrets,
but bring a message of help to your lord,
the leader of the Danes.

It is said in sorrowful tales
that a skulking scourge
stalks the moor-lands by night,
unlocks scathe and slaughter
and unheard-of ruin.
I offer these words to Hrothgar
as serious counsel,
and bring a way for this wise ruler
to win over death-filled days.
A way to end sorrow and torment,
to find revenge and healing,
and put away heart-pain in this helpless land.
Unless he heeds me,
he and his people
are doomed to darkness and grief
and long banishment
from the bright halls of Heorot."

Unafraid, the coast-watcher,
a hardy horseman, spoke:
"A worthy warden
deftly knows words and deeds.
You speak well with words of praise
for the Lord of the Danes,
so I will allow you and your men
to keep your armor.
I will lead you and your troops
with your shields and tall helmets
to the hall you seek.
I will tell my kin-thanes
to guard your ring-necked ship,

its prow at rest upon our shore,

until it returns over the sea-streams

bearing the best among you homeward.

All beloved warriors

who survive the battle rush

will ride the sea-foam

back to the Weder-mark."

The oath-sworn shieldmen

followed the land-guard,

and left their ship behind

on the shore riding its ropes,

a broad-bosomed craft at anchor fast.

Life-defending helmets gleamed,

polished boar-shapes

shone over bright cheek-guards

made of gold both fierce and fire-hardened.

With war-ready hearts

the sea-soldiers hurried,

marched side-by-side

until they glimpsed Heorot,

glorious and gold-wreathed,

Hrothgar's timbered gift hall

that overtopped all others near and far.

Then the warden of the coast

turned his horse and spoke to the Geats:

"It is time I return to the sea-cliffs

and keep watch

for any who seek to do us harm.

May Odin give you good luck in battle.

Fare well, bold warriors."

The shining stone-made street

stretched before them and the men set out.

War byrnies shone,

shimmering with hard hand-linked ring-iron.

The bright armor

sang of battle

as the men marched to the high hall

in their grim gear.

Sea-weary, they set their shields

firmly against the building's wall,

ranked their spears together

in a gray-tipped

ash-wood forest of death-staves,

then bent to the bench

with the clear ringing of byrnies,

warrior's war-clothes.

So rested the Geats,

an iron troop wealthy with weapons.

A king's-thane came from inside

and stood before them, saying:

    "I am Wulfgar,

    thane-friend of the lord of the Scyldings.

    Where do you come from

    with your plated shields,

    gray sarks, grim helmets,

    and your hoard of war-woods?

I have not seen many bolder looking men.

I think you travel from bravery, not exile,

seeking Hrothgar from heart-urge."

The courageous prince

and proud Weather-Geat, spoke:

"We are shield-men of mighty Hygelac.

Beowulf is my name.

I come to greet the son of Halfdane,

king of these lands.

I bring him hope-words if he will see us,

and will tell him, so good a man,

why we sailed westward to his mead-hall."

Wulfgar, the Wendels' chieftain

famed for his courage,

war-skill and wisdom, spoke:

"I will stand before the high-seat

and greet the gift-throne,

give lord Hrothgar your name

and tell him you bring words of help.

I will ask if he will see you,

and will bear his answer back here to you."

He entered the hall

where sat the age-hoary Hrothgar

with his war-band.

Skilled in the customs

of the lords of the North,

Wulfgar strode quickly

to the king's shoulder

and spoke to his friend-lord:

"Here have come strangers
from over the sea-fields,
wave-riders from Geat-land.
The greatest of them, I deem,
is named Beowulf.
They wish to greet you
and trade words with you,
and ask you not to refuse them your hospitality,
lord Hrothgar.
By their war-gear,
these are worthy men
who serve a mighty king."

Hrothgar, Scylding-helm answered:
"I knew him from a youth,
and his father, Ecgtheow,
who gave Hrethel, a Geat-lord,
his only daughter.
Beowulf is Ecgtheow's heir
and has come to seek me,
his father's loyal friend.
It is said
he has the strength of thirty thanes
in his hand-grip,
and has won much battle-fame.
Odin, our war-father, has sent him
to us, the West-Danes,
as hope against Grendel's terror.
I will offer that good man treasure
for his daring.
Go now,

tell him and his thanes

we welcome them to the Danish nation."

Wulfgar returned to the doors of Heorot

and opened them.

He said:

"My victory-lord commands me to say that

he knows your lineage, and you are come to him

hard-minded over the sea-swells

and are here welcome.

Now you may pass

in your war-gear and masked helmets

to see Hrothgar

but let your battle-shields and slaughter-shafts

rest here until your words are done."

Then the mighty man arose

with his warriors around him,

a sturdy thanes' band.

Some stayed behind to guard war-weapons

as their hardy leader had bade.

The others hurried together following Wulfgar

as he guided them under Heorot's roof.

Beowulf, in his shining byrnie,

bright armor-net woven by smith's skill,

hailed the king of the Danes:

"Be you well, Hrothgar!

I am Hygelac's kinsman and thane.

I have done many great deeds in my youth.

Grendel's deceitful slaughter-game

is well known in my country.

Seafarers say that when night falls

and heaven's brightness is hidden,

this hall,

the finest of buildings for all warriors,

stands idle and useless.

The best of my people, wise-minded men,

advised me to come here to you,

lord Hrothgar.

They know my mighty strength.

They saw it for themselves

when I came from battles

stained with enemy-blood.

They saw it when I bound five

and destroyed giants' kin.

In sea-waves I slew monsters by night

and suffered gnawing torment.

I avenged Wederas' wrongs

—all troubles they had asked for—

and ground down grim foes.

Now I shall fight alone

against Grendel the fiend-monster.

Lord of the Bright-Danes

and shield of the Scyldings,

now that I have come this far,

do not refuse me this one request:

My oath-sworn band of war-friends and I

shall cleanse Heorot.

We have also heard

that this monster in his raging

is not harmed by weapons.

So I also

—my liege lord Hygelac

may in his heart laugh at this—

will scorn sword and broad shield.

With my hand-grip only

I will struggle foe against foe

and let Fate decide

which of us will be taken by death.

Un-afraid in this war-hall,

Grendel will think

to eat up Geats' people

as often and easily as he did

the muscle of noble Danish men.

You will not need to shroud my head

if he drenches me in gore

and death takes me.

If the lone-prowler,

unlamenting in his moor-lair,

bears my bloody corpse away to feast upon,

you will not need

to grieve long over my body's welfare.

If death takes me, I ask only

that you send to Hygelac

this best of battle-shrouds

and finest of war-garments,

my bone-house armor.

It is Hrethel's legacy,

handwork of Weland the smith.

Fate always goes as she must!"

Hrothgar spoke, helm of the Scyldings:

    "My friend Beowulf,

for war and for favor

you have come to us.

Your father, Ecgtheow,

slew Heatholaf of the Wylfings

with his own hand

and began a long feud.

He could neither pay wergild,

nor find shelter amongst the Wederas' kin,

so he sought the South-Danes,

the Honor-Scyldings,

over the waves.

In my youth, I was king of that people

and held that precious kingdom,

the hoard-fort of heroes,

because my elder brother

Heorogar,

son of Halfdane, died.

He was better than I.

I sent treasured heirlooms to the Wylfings

over the water's ridge

and settled the feud-debt,

so Ecgtheow swore oaths to me.

It sorrows me to speak to any man

about the hurt and the shame

Grendel has caused me

with his hate-thoughts,

his hall-ravaging—

my war band is waned,

swept away by Fate in the fiend's slaughter.

Too many times,

drunk on beer or ale, kin-thanes vowed

to stay Grendel's in-rushes
with their grim swords.
Yet, when morning came
this great house
had been stained with death once more.
When the day lightened,
all the bench-woods
were slicked with blood
and the floors were marred
with slaughter-tracks.
Friends were made fewer
and beloved kin-thanes were gone,
taken away by death.
But sit now to feast and untie your thoughts,
tell men of your victory-fame as your heart urges."

Then room was made for the Geat-men
on the bench in the beer-hall
and the strong-hearted
went to sit down there together,
proud in their prowess.
A thane bearing an ale-cup poured bright drink.
A poet's song rose, clear in Heorot.
There was heroes' high hall-joy
in the large host of Danes and Wederas.
Unferth, Ecglaf's son, sitting at Hrothgar's feet,
felt his bitterness rise up
because Beowulf did not allow
that any other man
on middle-earth

had done braver deeds than he had.

He unbound his battle-words:

    "Are you the Beowulf who fought with Breca,

    raced swimming on the broad sea,

    tested the oceans

    with your foolish boasts

    and risked lives in deep water?

    No man, friend or foe, could prevent you

    from that childish dare

    when you swam in the sea.

    There you embraced tide-streams

    and measured sea-roads,

    thrashed your arms

    and glided over the ocean.

    Surging water welled in winter swells.

    You strove for seven nights

    in the wide water-grasp,

    but Breca bested you in swimming,

    he had more strength.

    The sea cast him up in the morning-time

    on the coast of the Heatho-Reams

    and from there

    he sought the sweet homeland

    dear to his people, the Brondings,

    a fine stronghold

    where he had kin,

    fortress and rings.

    Breca, son of Beanstan,

    truly kept his boast with you.

    Because of that venture,

even though you have survived
other battle-clashes elsewhere,
I expect worse results from you
if you dare a night-long wait
for Grendel's grim war-game."

Beowulf spoke, Ecgtheow's son:
"Listen to me, my friend Unferth,
you are drunk on much beer.
You have spoken of Breca
and told us about his venture.
I claim, truthfully,
that I had the greater sea-strength
and had more hardships in the waves
than any other man.
Breca and I agreed
—both of us lads still in our youth—
that we would
risk our lives out on the ocean
and so we did.
Thinking to defend ourselves against whales
we carried unsheathed swords
 hard in our hands when we went into the sea.
We did not float far from each other.
Together on the sea we spent a five-night span
until we were separated by the current
in heaving seas and coldest of weathers.
Night darkened,
and the battle-keen north-wind
blew against us
as we turned into the cruel waves.

Then the anger of the sea-fishes was stirred up,

but my gold-crested body-sark,

my hard hand-linked battle-dress,

lay on my breast

and protected me against them.

I was dragged to the depths

by a fierce foe-scather

and firmly held in its grim grasp,

yet luck was with me

and I pierced the monster

with my battle-blade.

I destroyed the mighty sea-beast

through the strength in my hand.

After that, savage water-monsters

threatened me many times.

I served them well with my precious blade,

as was fitting,

and those sea-fiends had no feast-joy.

They did not devour me,

but lay on the sea-floor,

wounded and suffering.

In the morning

the sea cast them up on the sand

in sweet sword-sleep,

and since then never again on steep water

did they halt the course

of any sea-farer.

When light from Odin's bright beacon

came from the east,

the waves subsided

and I saw

the headlands' wind-swept rock-walls.
Fate often spares the undoomed man
when his heart endures.
Luck was with me,
for with my sword I killed nine monsters.
I have never heard under heaven's hollow
of a harder fight,
nor on the tide-streams
a more hard-pressed man.
I escaped the foes' grasp alive,
weary from my turmoil.
Then the sea swept me off
in its wallowing waves and flooding current
to the land of the Lapps.
I have never heard tell
of any such deadly combats
for you, Unferth.
Neither you nor Breca,
in battle-play, has ever
performed so bold a deed
with a shining sword
—not that I boast much—
but you, Unferth, you killed
your brothers, your close kinsmen.
For that you will answer to Hel,
though you might think otherwise in your mind.
I tell you truly, son of Ecglaf,
that Grendel, the terrible monster,
would never have done so many grim deeds
to your leader,
or hurts in Heorot,

if your courage, your heart,

were so battle-fierce

as you yourself say it is.

The fiend has found

he has no need to fear

a terrible sword-storm from your nation

of Victory-Scyldings;

he takes his forced toll

and shows pity to none

in the nation of Danes.

He takes pleasure,

slays and slices,

because he expects no fight

from the Spear-Danes.

But I will show him Geat-strength and courage

before long now.

I will offer him battle.

When the sun

bright-clothed in morning-light from the south

shines over mens' sons,

Grendel, who has exulted

over his destruction to this mead-hall

will be gone."

Hrothgar, old-haired and war-brave,

chief of the Bright- Danes,

knew then that Beowulf,

the best of warriors, spoke truly.

He would aid his people.

Noise of heroes' laughter and warriors' joy

resounded in Heorot.

Then Wealhtheow, Hrothgar's queen,

walked forth

adorned in gold and mindful of kindness.

The noble lady welcomed the hall-warriors

and handed the shining mead-cup

first to Hrothgar, her husband

and land-protector of the East-Danes,

loved by his nation,

bidding him to be happy at the beer-taking.

The victory-king took delight

in feasting and in the mead-cup.

Then the Lady of the Helmings went among them,

veterans and youths alike,

and handed golden beakers to each,

until time came that the ring-adorned queen,

in excellent spirits, stood before Beowulf

with the mead-bowl in her hand.

She greeted the Geats' chief,

and with wise words thanked Odin

for granting her wish that a warrior would come

to bring the nation relief

from the fiend's hate-hot harrying.

Beowulf, slaughter-fierce warrior,

took the costly vessel from Wealhtheow

and gave voice, eager for the coming combat:

    "When I put out on the ocean,

      settled in a sea-boat with my war-band,

I intended

to fittingly fulfill the Dane-folk's wishes

or fall in slaughter,

fixed fast in the foe's grip.

I vowed to finish this daring deed

or else

endure my death-day

in this mead-hall."

The gold-adorned woman, noble folk-queen,

liked well the Geat's boast-speech

and went to sit by her lord.

As before,

happy people spoke bold words inside the hall,

the victory-folk's feast-clamour,

and then before long

Hrothgar, son of Halfdane,

wished to seek his evening rest.

When the sun's light darkened

and night fell,

he knew the monster

had readied another evening slaughter,

and soon the shadow-helm's shape

would come sliding dark under the clouds.

The company rose up.

Each man greeted the other,

and Hrothgar wished Beowulf

good luck and rule of the wine hall.

Then the Danish king said:

"Never have I entrusted Heorot to any man
since I raised this strong-hall of the Danes
by hand and shield—save to you.
Hold and guard this most noble house now;
keep valor in your mind
and show strong war-skills against the foe.
If you endure this courage-deed alive,
you will suffer no lack of treasure."

Then Hrothgar, defender of the Scyldings,
went out from the hall with his heroes' band
to seek Wealhtheow, his queen, as bed-mate.
Odin Allfather had provided the Scyldings
with a mighty house-guard against Grendel.
Beowulf, bold warrior, held for the Danish king
the special task of monster-guard,
as men have heard.
The Geat-leader gladly trusted
in his own mighty strength
and favor from Odin.
Beowulf removed from himself
his iron byrnie and his high helmet,
handed his treasured sword to his servant-thane
and commanded him to guard well his battle-gear.
Before he lay down to sleep, the good man,
Beowulf the Geat,
spoke more boast words:

"I do not reckon my war-strength
is weaker in battle-deeds

than is Grendel's
—he has no war-skills,
he may strike back at me,
 he may even hack at my shield,
 though he is more famous for
deceit and deadly tricks—
so I will not weary him with my sword
or deprive him of life, though I surely could.
Since he seeks war without weapons,
we will also forsake our swords this night,
and let Fate decide
which of us will be given war-honor."

Then Beowulf, battle-bold man,
bent to his bolster to rest
with many a sturdy sea-thane in hall-sleep
settled around him.
No man thought
he would ever again return to his loved country,
his own folk or noble fort
where he once was nurtured,
for they had all heard that in this wine-hall
the foe had already destroyed
far too many Danes in bloody death.
But success would come to the Wederas' men
in their war-webs,
and they would take joy in their prowess,
overcoming the slaughter-fiend
through one man's strength, one man's might.

In the darkest heart of night

the Shadow-walker left his lair.

Swift-shooting bowmen,

who kept the horn-gabled house safe, slept,

all but one.

It was long known

that if Odin did not allow the strife

to go their way,

they could never

drag the man-scather

under the shadows by themselves.

But one watched for the foe with building anger,

waiting in rising rage

for the outcome of the battle.

Then from the moor under the mist-hills

came Grendel, slaughter-bent,

fully intending to snare a warrior

in the high hall.

He waded under clouds

until he clearly sighted the wine-hall,

the gold-glimmering glee-house of men.

This was not the first time

he had sought Hrothgar's home,

but never in his life-days,

before or since,

would he ever

find harder luck

or a hardier hall-thane in wait.

Creeping closer,

the creature stood outside the building,

cut off from all its joy.

Full of rage, he put his hands to the door

and burst open its iron bands,

ripped apart the building's mouth.

He passed quickly into the high hall,

hate-treading across the shining floor,

eyes a-flame with ghastly light.

He saw many warriors together,

a sleeping kin-troop,

a host of soldiers,

and his heart laughed—

he had chanced upon a feast-meal.

Before the day broke, he,

dreadful monster,

would tear from every man

his life and limbs.

He could not know

that after this night

it would never again

be his fate to devour any man.

Hygelac's powerful kinsman

waited and watched to see how the killer

made his swift attacks.

The monster did not delay

but snatched a sleeping warrior

and slashed unhindered,

bit through bone-locks,

drank vein-blood,

and gorged great chunks.

Soon he had swallowed up an entire man,

everything, even feet and hands.

Then the fiend stepped toward Beowulf

and reached for him with an open-palm,

took with his hand

the courageous warrior at rest.

In that moment, the best of Geats

understood the malice-maker's thoughts

and clasped tight the criminal's arm,

and the shadow-stalker knew

his strength had met its match,

knew he had never met

in middle-earth or the world's expanse

a harder hand-grip in any other man.

His heart turned craven at his core

and he wished for quick escape,

yearned to flee into the dark

and seek the demons' throng.

Heorot's welcome was not as it had been.

Beowulf remembered his evening boast-speech

and leaped to his feet.

He grasped the shadow-walker more firmly.

The monster tried to pull away,

fingers bursting,

but Beowulf would not let go.

Grendel sought to flee and find refuge

in fen-lairs, if he might, farther away.

This was a bitter journey

the beast had made to Heorot.

The clan-hall thundered

and a deadly terror

fell upon the Danes and the camp dwellers,

the bold heroes and all the warriors,

as Beowulf and Grendel battled

full of rage and loathing.

The building resounded.

The great wonder was that the famed hall

withstood the battle-fighters' fury,

but it had been firmly built

with iron bonding inside and out

and that fair feast-hall did not fall to earth.

As I heard,

many gold-bright mead-benches were

broken up where the two foes struggled.

It had never been thought

by the wise Scyldings

that any man, brilliant and bone-adorned,

might batter or bring down Heorot

unless fire's flames

should wreath its golden gables

in deadly embrace.

It was then that a sound arose

like nothing ever heard before,

and a fierce dread

welled up in Hrothgar's host.

All heard the wailing from the hall—Grendel,

Hel's captive, screaming his death-song.

Beowulf, strongest of Geats,

held fast the fiend in his mighty hand-grip.

Not for any cause, nor to any man,

would Earl Hrothgar's hall-guard

release this lethal guest alive.

Many of Beowulf's warriors

carried ancient swords

and wished to protect, if they could,

their prince-lord's life,

aid their chieftain.

They did not know

when they joined the conflict

that no blade on earth,

no matter

whose battle-hard hand wielded it,

could wound the soul-scather,

for Grendel had made useless by a spell

every sword-edge, every victory-weapon.

The man-slayer's life-end on this day

would be wretched,

his departing spirit

would travel far-off

into the dread-realm of fiends.

Grendel, who had before committed

many crimes

and mind miseries on mankind,

suddenly found that his body

would not obey him.

Hygelac's keen kinsman

had him in the greatest of grips.

A mortal wound

split open the monster's shoulder.

Sinews sprang apart and bone-locks burst.

Beowulf was given war-glory,

fate had chosen him the victor.

One-armed and life-sick

Grendel fled under the fen-slopes

to seek his joyless home.

The end of his life had come,

his day-count would be finished.

Then for the Danes

came longed-for peace after the death-clash.

He who had first come from afar,

shrewd and strong-hearted

to Hrothgar's hall,

had rescued it from ruin.

Beowulf had fulfilled his vow

to the East-Danes' leader.

He rejoiced in the night's work,

in his courage-deeds.

He had removed Scylding anguish,

soothed the bitter sorrow

they had long suffered

in stern duress, no un-little torment.

Then, beneath the eaves

of Heorot's spacious roof,

the battle-brave man

hung up the token of his victory

—Grendel's grim remainder—

hand, arm, and shoulder, all one.

In the morning, as I have heard,

many warriors and famed folk-chiefs

fared from far and near,

through wide ways,

to survey the grim wonder in the gift hall

and to track the foe's footprints.

Sharp-eyed soldiers on steeds

followed the weary-hearted fiend's

blood-wet path

from Heorot

toward the marsh-mere,

where, driven back doomed and defeated,

Grendel had left his death-tracks.

The soldiers did not sorrow.

In the mere-water, blood mingled with scalding gore

and welled with seething sword-sweat.

Death-doomed and deprived of all joy,

Grendel had hidden in his fen-lair.

He yielded up his life and Hel enfolded him.

Then the warriors, old and young,

turned back toward Heorot with glad joy,

harriers on horses.

As they rode they told and re-told

the story of Beowulf's triumph,

and many often said that south or north,

between the seas

in the whole wide earth,

under the sky's expanse,

there was no one more fitting,

no shield-fighter worthier, of the kingdom.

No one the least

held glad Hrothgar to blame

for the Grendel-feud,

for he was their friend-lord,

and a good king.

At times, where to them the earth-roads

seemed easy and most well known,

the returning warriors would race in contest

and let their horses gallop.

At other times, the king's word-thane

recalled songs

or remembered ancient stories.

With practiced skill

he created new songs

about the feat of Beowulf,

artfully weaving

a tale in keeping

with his wondrous word-hoard.

Likewise,

the thane sang the saga of Sigmund,

Wael's son, telling them

of that hero's wonders and daring deeds,

his strifes and wide-faring journeys,

his feuds and feats of arms.

Sigmund's deeds

were unknown to many mens' sons,

except Fitela, his nephew,

who often fared far with him.

Nephew and uncle spoke together often,

for in every spear-battle

they were shield-comrades

and had slain many giants' kin with their swords.

After Sigmund's death-day,

no little fame sprang up for him.

The battle-tested warrior had slain a serpent,

hoard's guardian,

under the gray stone.

Wael's son ventured the fearless deed alone,

for Fitela was not with him that day.

By luck the lordly iron of his slaughter-sword

pierced the serpent through,

pinned him fast against the wall,

and the dragon died in his earth-den.

Sigmund, serpent-slayer,

broke into the guard-less ring-hoard

with pleasure and loaded up

the bosom of his boat with glimmering gold.

Sigmund, monster-slayer

and warriors' protector,

was the most famous of all heroes

for his courage deeds

—by which he had prospered.

Not like Heremod, whose failed heroism

had ceased in strength and spirit.

Heremod, a Jutish king,

was deceived into following his foes' power.

He fell from favor with his kin-thanes

and was swiftly sent away into exile.

Lamed by his growing grief,

he became a living sorrow to his people,

to all his followers.

In earlier days, better days,

many wise men had trusted him

to give them ring-gifts for their service

but he would not.

So all hoped

that Heremod's son would prosper

and assume the father's rank,

rule the people well, hoard and stronghold,

a heroes' kingdom, homeland of Scyldings.

Beowulf, kinsman of Hygelac,

won much favor from mens' sons,

but Heremod's violence consumed him.

Hrothgar's warriors sped on,

following fallow tracks

as morning's light shifted, hurrying the day.

At Heorot, the high hall,

many soldiers came to see the strange wonder.

So too did the king himself.

He came from the bride-bower,

glorious ring-hoards' guard

with his war-band.

Wealhtheow, his queen,

with her maidens' company,

paced the mead-path beside him.

Hrothgar, lord of the Danes,

stood on the steps beneath the steep roof

of the gold-bright hall

and looked up to where hung

the slaughterer's hand,

and spoke:

"For this sight,

we make swift and joyous thanks to Odin-Allfather!

I suffered much spite and grief from Grendel.

Now may the gods

always give us such victory-luck as this.

It was not long ago when this hall,

most splendid house,

stood sword-gory and marked by blood-feud.

I could not hope to pay wergild

for all the deaths done here.

Woe spread, scattered far and wide,

for all wise men who no longer believed

they could protect this nation's stronghold

from foes, fiends, and evil spirits.

But now this warrior

has performed a deed

which we might never have dreamed of

in our woe.

Listen now!

I say whichever woman among mankind

bore this man,

if she yet lives,

the All-father was gracious to her in child-bearing.

Beowulf, best of men, I say to you

I will love you as a son always.

Keep well this new kinship from now on.

If I have my way,

you will never lack for any worldly wishes.

Very often I have granted hoard-honor

to humbler men for lesser deeds,

men who were inferior at fighting.

By your deeds you have ensured for yourself

that your fame will live forever.

May Odin always reward you well, as he just now did."

Beowulf spoke, son of Ecgtheow:

"We Geats dared this brave deed

with great good-will

and boldly set ourselves

against the strength of an unknown foe.

I wish you had seen the shadow-walker,

weary in death.

I took him quickly in my hard hand-clasp,

thinking to bind him to his slaughter-bed,

struggling for his life,

hold him fast in my death-grip

lest he get away.

But it was not my fate

to stop the fiend from escaping,

nor hold that life-enemy back.

He was too strong, a most-mighty foe.

Yet as he ran away,

he left with me his life-pledge

—hand, arm and shoulder—

which bought the wretched creature

no respite.

That loathed killer

no longer lives,

his life taken by the great wound
from my battle-grasp.
Now he is tightly held,
fatally fettered, in Hel's mighty embrace,
a fitting fate for such a one."
Unferth, son of Ecglaf,
was made less wordy
in his boasting against Beowulf's strength
as the noble men gazed
on proof of the Geat-earl's prowess:
Grendel's hand hung up under the high roof,
the heathen's hand-claw,
the battle-creature's terrible talons
bearing a nail hard as hammered iron
at the front of each fiend-finger.
People said they had heard
that the bloody battle-arm could not be hurt
by even the oldest and truest iron.
Then the order went out
to adorn Heorot's hall within,
and many men and women
made ready the wine-house guest-hall.
The weavings on the walls shone gold-bright,
many wonder-sights for all the people
who take pleasure in such things to see.
Though secured with iron-bonds
the bright building had been badly broken,
the sanctuary burst apart.

Only the roof remained entirely sound

after the monster,

guilty of grim deeds and despairing of life,

turned and fled.

It is not easy to flee from death

—no matter who tries—

and when compelled by need,

every earth-dweller

must seek the prepared place,

a fixed death bed where his body

will long-sleep after feasting.

At last came the time and hour

when Halfdane's son

wished to partake of the feast

and went to the hall.

I have never heard the host

greet their treasure-giver with greater joy.

Then the fame-wielders

and stout-hearted hearth-kin

bent to the bench,

rejoiced at the feast

and fittingly received many mead-cups.

Hrothgar and Hrothulf his nephew

also shared their joy in the hall.

Heorot was filled with friends.

No traitor-deeds had yet

come to the Folk-Scyldings.

Then Hrothgar gave to Beowulf

a braided battle-banner woven with gold,

a bright byrnie,

and a helm, as victory's reward.

Woven wires wound about the helmet's roof

to guard the warrior's head,

wreathing the outside rim

so that no well-honed sword

would scathe him when slaughter-seekers

clash in the shield-wall of war.

Beowulf gladly drank his cup

with no need to feel shame

among Heorot's warriors

for accepting these rich fee-gifts.

I have not heard of gold or treasures

 given to men on the ale-benches

in a friendlier way.

Then Hrothgar, the earls' defender,

ordered eight gold-bridled horses

to be led in under the ramparts of Heorot.

One of them

bore Hrothgar's bright saddle

set with jewels,

the high-king's battle seat

whenever the son of Halfdane

wished to join in swords' play.

The far-famed ruler's war-skill

had never failed

when corpses were falling.

Into Beowulf's possession

passed Hrothgar's generous gifts,

horses and weapons in all their brightness.

The Scylding lord told him to enjoy them well.

Thus the famed chieftain,

hoard-guard of heroes,

paid for the battle-clash

with a generous gift

of horses and treasures,

and no truth-telling man

could find fault with him.

Hrothgar also gave

treasures and heirlooms to each warrior

who had travelled the brine-path

with Beowulf and sat beside him

on the mead-bench.

Then he commanded that wergild be paid

for the first Geat-man

Grendel had killed in his malice.

The soul-slayer would have claimed more,

but Odin's war-wisdom

and Beowulf's courage

prevented that fate.

Fate controls mankind, as it ever has.

For this reason, the prudent man is mindful of it,

understanding that he who enjoys this world

shall endure much good and evil

in these strife-filled days.

Then were song and music

joined together before Halfdane's battle-leader.

Hrothgar's bard on the mead-bench

strummed the glee-wood

and began an oft-told tale of Finn's heirs:

It was the fate of Hnaef the Scylding,

Half-Dane hero,

to fall on the Frisian field

when sudden war came upon them

However Hildeburh, his sister,

had no need to praise the Jutes' loyalty.

Guiltless, she was bereft of two loved ones

who opposed each other in the shield play,

son and brother,

and both fell to spear wounds.

That was an un-happy woman.

Not without cause

did Hildeburh mourn fate's choice

when morning came,

for where formerly

she had beheld her world's joy

she could now see

the corpses of her beloveds under the sky.

That war destroyed all Finn's thanes

save a few,

so that he might not in that meeting-place

win further clash with Hengest,

nor drive out the survivors—

war's wretched remnant.

He offered peace-terms

and cleared out another

hearth, hall, and high seat

so that he and Hengest might share rule.

Every day, Finn, Folcwalda's son,

honored Hengest's band of Danes with rings,

even such treasure-store of hoard-gold

as he would give to his own Frisian tribe

in the beer-hall.

Both sides agreed to a vow of peace.

With firm promise

Finn swore oaths to Hengest.

He vowed that in honor,

and by wise men's judgment

he would restrain his woeful remnant

so that no man among them

should break the treaty by words or deeds,

nor would any of his men

taunt Hnaef's warriors,

who, now lordless,

were forced

to follow the slayer of their own ring-giver.

He said that if any Frisian

reminded the Danes of the blood-feud

to enrage them,

all such insults

should be settled by the sword's edge.

After that, Hnaef's bale-fire was prepared

and gold was fetched from the home's hoard.

The War-Scyldings' best warrior

was readied on the pyre.

His battle-stained sark

and its iron-hard boar symbol

had been washed in waves of blood.

Hnaef died a hero's death,

destroyed by his wounds.

Likewise,

many great men

had fallen in that shield-play.

Hildeburh ordered her son's corpse

to be placed beside her dead brother,

the boy's uncle,

consigned to those same flames

and his bone-house burned.

As the slaughter-fire flared up she mourned,

bewailing her loss with sorrow-filled laments.

Sorrow-smoke soared into the clouds,

rose up to the sky from the heaped funeral-fire

as flames roared loud in the death-mound.

Heads melted,

wound-gates burst

when blood gushed out

through all the hate-bites in the bodies.

The blaze, greediest of guests,

swallowed all the battle-warriors

taken from both peoples

as their glory rose skyward in the hot wind.

Then the fighters, bereft of friends,

returned

to the hearths, homes and high-fort of Frisia.

Hengest, still slaughter-stained,

spent the winter with Finn

yearning for his own land,

though he could not sail his ring-prowed ship

on the sea where winter-locked waves

fought storm-surges

and wrestled with the wind.

Ice-bound water

kept sailors close to the hearth

until another year came in the land,

as it still does,

for those

who observe the seasons' glory-bright weathers.

Winter was gone, earth's breast turned fair;

and the exile-guest yearned

to set out from Frisia

even though his mind

dwelled more on grief-revenge

than the sea-path.

He contrived a strife-clash

and used his war-iron

to remind the Jutes' sons of their former feud.

Then Hengest did not deny the world's counsel

when Hunlaf's son placed a gleaming blade,

the finest battle flame, in his lap

Those iron-edges

were well-known among the Jutes.

Across the sail-road in Jutland,

Guthlaf and Oslaf heard the sorrow-song

of Hnaef's fall.

They tallied woes' losses

and made swift sea-journey to Frisia.

No heart can restrain a battle-eager spirit.

Hengest opened Finn's gates to them

and thus Finn in his turn

received the enemy's cruel sword-slaughter

in his own home.

The hall was reddened with foes' life-endings.

Finn, too, was slain,

the king with his company,

and Hildeburh his queen was seized.

Then for recompense,

the Scylding shield-warriors

laid claim to all Finn's house-goods

they could find

—jewels, treasure-gems, heirloom weapons—

and loaded the hoard into the ships.

Once more out on the sea-path

they ferried noble Hildeburh back to the Danes,

back to her own people.

The glee-man

ended his song of Finn and the Frisian

and the sound of hall-joy rose up,

bright bench-noise rang clearly,

and cup-bearers

served wine from wondrous vessels.

Wearing a gold neck ring,

Wealhtheow walked forth

to where Hrothgar and Hrothulf sat,

two good men, uncle and nephew;

united in kinship, each to the other true.

Also Unferth, word-wielder,

sat at the feet of the lord of Scyldings.

Though uncle and nephew trusted him

and said he had much courage,

they knew in sword-clashes

he was not respectful to his kin.

Wealhtheow spoke, lady of the Scyldings:

"My noble lord Hrothgar, treasure-giver,
receive this cup.
You joyfully spoke gentle words
to these great battle-Geats
as a man ought to do.
Be gracious to the Geat-heroes
and mindful with gifts,
give them gold from your hoard,
old treasures you possess
from near and far.
I have heard it said
you wished to have this warrior,
Beowulf,
as a son because he cleansed Heorot
and made the ring-hall bright once more.
Great gold-friend, take joy in this glory
while you may
but when you go forth to meet your death
in your fate-appointed time,
make your own kinsmen
heirs to your people and your kingdom.
Gracious Hrothulf, you know
your uncle Hrothgar
will hold the youths in honor
if you find death earlier than he,
and dear Hrothgar,
we know your nephew Hrothulf
will repay our children with good,
if he remembers all the favors
we bestowed upon him in his youth."

Then she turned to the bench

where sat her sons Hrethric and Hrothmund

with other heroes' sons, the youth-band together.

In their company

sat good Beowulf of the Geats.

The cup was carried to him

and words of friendship

were lavished upon him,

twisted gold kindly offered—

two arm-ornaments, a robe and rings,

and the largest neck-ring I have seen

since Hama bore off

the glorious Brosings' necklace

to the shining stronghold.

No neck jewel under the sky

had ever been more famed

in the hoard-treasures of heroes.

It is said that it was Freya's ornament,

but Hama took that jewel and its casket, too,

a theft that earned him the hatred

of Eormenric, king of the Goths.

He fled that king's wrath.

On the last raid of his life,

Hygelac the Geat

grand-son of Swerting,

wore that neck-ring

over the waves' bowl

and defended it under his own banner.

Arrogant in his power,

he began a feud with the Frisians,

but Fate overwhelmed the powerful war-king

and he fell beneath his shield,

a kingly price for pride.

After Hygelac fell in the slaughter,

Geat corpses filled the blood-field,

and less-powerful war-men

plundered the slain.

Hygelac's body, breast-armor,

and that neck-jewel, together,

passed into the hands of the Franks.

Heorot resounded with mead-joy.

Wealhtheow spoke before the soldiers

and said,

    "Enjoy this ring, Beowulf, beloved warrior,

    with good luck,

    and use this robe, nation's treasure,

    to thrive well.

    Prove yourself by strength,

    and to these lads, my sons,

    be kind in counsels.

    I will reward you for that.

    You have achieved praise from nations

    far and near, all and forever,

    as widely as the seas surround us

    from wind-yard to cliff-walls.

While you live,

be happy, lordly man!

I wish you well with treasure-riches.

To my sons,

be you gentle in deeds!

Every man here is true to the other,

merciful in mind and loyal to his liege-lord.

The thanes are united.

The nation, this drink-cheered host,

does as I bid."

Wealhtheow went then to her seat.

There followed the finest feast,

men drank wine and told tales.

They were not thinking of Fate

or of dire destiny,

as it often is when heroes are at peace.

Evening came

and Hrothgar went to his bower,

the ruler to rest.

A host of men guarded the hall as always.

They bared the bench-wood

and spread bedding and bolsters on the floor.

One beer-warrior among them,

death-doomed,

lay down in his hall-bed.

Near the head of each man,

benches bore battle-shields,

bright board-wood.

Next to the war-boards

rested boar-crested helmets,

ringed byrnies, and spear-shafts sturdy.

Their custom was

to always be prepared for war

whether at home or out harrying,

at all such times as need arose for their

ring-lord.

The nation was worthy of its warriors.

The soldiers sank then into sleep.

One paid sorely for his evening rest,

as had very often happened to many others

since Grendel first

guarded the gold-hall and filled it with evil

until his death-day claimed him.

What would soon become clear

and well-known to men

was that a fiend-avenger

still lived,

a loathsome wight

full of long-held war-grief—Grendel's mother.

The vile monster-queen, a wretched creature,

mourned her demon spawn

who had met his fate at Heorot

when he found a warrior waiting.

From that battle Grendel, mankind's foe,

fled, wounded,

to seek his death-house,

and his mother,

greedy for slaughter, went forward

with grieving step to avenge her son's death.

She came to Heorot,

where Ring-Danes slept throughout the hall.

Beowulf was not there, for earlier,

after the treasure-giving,

he had been given another bower.

When Grendel's mother crept into the hall

it was a return

to once-known terror for the soldiers.

Her horror was less by just as much

as is woman's strength,

woman's war-power, to a man's,

and his weapons

—blade-bound, boar-crested,

blood-stained and hammer-forged,

edges sharp and deadly—

compared to her shears.

The singing of hard-edged swords

pulled from sheaths

sang throughout the hall

when they first saw the she-beast,

many broad shields

were gripped in war-scarred hands.

But there was no need for helmets,

nor broad battle-byrnies,

for too-soon seen,

the foul fiend rushed out of the hall

to save her life.

In her haste

she seized a warrior in her firm grip,

grasped Grendel's now-famous arm in all its gore,

and fled back to the fens.

The warrior she snatched from his bed

was Hrothgar's best-loved hero,

a sturdy shield-warrior, a glorious man.

It is a bad bargain

if each side must pay the price with a friend's life.

The good king, hoary-headed battle-man,

grieved with a sorrowing heart

when he learned his dearest thane was dead.

Beowulf, warrior-bold,

was quickly called to the Dane-lord's side,

and in the gray early light, the noble Geat,

best warrior, went with his shield-men

to where the wise king waited

wondering if for him

Fate would ever change.

Beowulf, war-worthy man,

crossed the floor through the hall-din

with his hand-chosen band,

approached Heorot's owner-lord and asked,

"What happened here after the feast-pleasure?"
Hrothgar spoke, helm of the Scyldings:
    "Do not speak of pleasure!
    Sorrow is renewed for this Danish nation.
    Aeschere is dead, Yrmenlaf's elder brother,
    the best of my men,
    keeper of my trust and my counsellor,
    my most dear shoulder-companion.
    He defended me in battle
    when armies clashed and boar-helmets broke.
    All men should be as Aeschere was,
    noble, loyal, and trustworthy.
    With her own hands, that she-monster,
    the errant slaughter-spirit,
    slew him in Heorot,
    but whither she returned
    to delight in her death-feast
    and terrible corpse-gloating,
    I do not know.
    Yesternight you killed Grendel
    because for too long
    he diminished and destroyed my nation.
    You met him in battle
    and your hard hand-grip tore off his arm.
    He fell in that fight,
    guilty of many life-hurts.
    But then came another, greater, man-scather,
    to avenge her son.
    By taking Aeschere, she has upheld the feud,
    as it may seem to many thanes

who weep in hard heart-grief with me,
their treasure-giver.
Low now lies the hand
which in all desires supported you.
I have heard from my people,
both land-dwellers and hall-sitters,
who say they saw two mighty marsh-steppers,
demon-spirits haunting the moors
and treading exile paths.
As clearly as they could see,
one of them was of a woman's likeness.
The other man-shaped, a miserable wretch,
larger than other men.
From ancient times
the earth-dwellers named him Grendel.
They did not know his father,
or whether he had been born of hidden spirits.
These fiends inhabit the wolf-slopes,
windy fells, and wild fen-paths
where mountain streams
dive downward beneath cliff-shadows,
making a flood under the earth.
The marsh-mere stands not far from here
in mile measures.
Hoary groves hang over the water
and tree roots tangle the shores.
 Branches over-shadow the depths.
At night
one may see deadly wonders out there—
flames burning in the flood.
No one is left of mens' sons

wise enough to know how deep it is.
If the hart, tough-horned heath-leaper
harried by hounds
and in flight from his hunters
seeks the forest,
he would gladly give up his life
and lie breath-less on the banks
before he sought that lake-water
to save his life.
It is not a pleasant place.
When the wind stirs dread-filled storms,
the mere throws up wave-swirls,
mounting higher
until the sky grays and the heavens weep.
Once more, Beowulf my friend,
the wisdom in this plight belongs to you alone.
You do not yet know the earth-paths
to the ghastly place
where you might find the fen-fiend:
seek her if you dare.
If Fate spares you
and you return from this battle,
I will reward you once more
with wealth, gleaming gold
and ancient treasures as I did before."
Beowulf spoke, son of Ecgtheow:
"Sorrow not, my wise lord!
It is better to avenge a friend
than to much mourn.
Each of us

must abide the end of our life in this world

and strive after glory before death.

Arise, now, kingdom's guardian,

let us go quickly

and search for Grendel's kin's spoor.

I swear to you this oath:

she will not be lost in cover,

nor in the earth's embrace,

nor in the mountain's wood,

nor in the ocean's depth,

wherever she seeks to hide.

Have patience this day

as you have always had for your miseries."

Hrothgar leaped up,

praising Odin for Beowulf's wise words.

Then the Dane-lord's horse,

his mare with a braided mane,

was bridled and brought forth.

In his bright war gear,

the wise chieftain rode, magnificent,

and his foot-troop of shield-bearers

marched beside.

Along the wood-swathes

the she-fiend's tracks were easily seen

where she had loped along the ground

over the murky moors,

carrying the lifeless corpse

of the dearest of all those kin-thanes

who had defended Heorot with Hrothgar.

Beowulf, hero's son,

followed the unknown course

over steep stone slopes,

narrow foot-ways,

and cramped single-paths;

past towering crags and monster-lairs

He chose a few kinsmen

and went ahead of the war-band

searching the earth

until all at once he saw mountain trees

hanging over hoary stones in a joyless forest.

Beneath the dripping branches,

the mere-water was boiling and blood-filled.

Then the pain each and every hero

had endured with their thane-lord deepened

for they found Aeschere's head

on the lake-side.

In the mere, the bloody flood welled up.

They stared at the hot gore

and dropped to the ground in grief.

In that same moment, their battle-horn

sang a fierce and urgent war-song

for they saw many snake-kinds cleaving the water,

strange sea-dragons

swimming the waves.

Many monsters

crawled up on the cliff-slopes

—serpents and wild beasts—

the same who in morningtimes

often carry out dire attacks on the sail-road.

The wrath-filled war-band attacked at speed,

their war-horn wailing.

A Geat warrior

speared a wave-serpent with his shaft-bow

so that hard in its heart the war-arrow stood.

The beast swam slower

and the battle-seekers

swiftly pursued

with barb-pointed boar-spears.

They stabbed the struggling beast

and dragged it out onto the mere-bank

where men

stared at the wondrous wave-thrasher,

a gruesome guest.

Beowulf geared himself in hero-armor,

in no way mourning his life.

His war-byrnie, woven by mighty hands,

broad and skill-bright,

would sheathe his bone-house,

and in the battle-grip of a foe's fierce strength

he would be un-scathed.

His white helm

would protect his head in the mere-depths.

It was wreathed with lordly bands

of gleaming gold,

wonderfully wrought in ancient days

and beset with boars' heads

so that no battle-blade

would bite through it.

Then Unferth, Hrothgar's word-warrior,

lent to Beowulf his hilt-sword Hrunting,

unequalled by any ancient treasure.

Its edges were iron-sharp,

hardened in battle-blood,

and the blade

was streaked with poisoned patterns.

It had never in any fight

betrayed the man who wielded it,

whoever dared venture

into the folk-place of foes.

This was not the first time

Hrunting must commit a courage deed.

When Unferth, son of Ecglaf,

lent that weapon to the better swordsman,

he did not dwell on what he had said before,

wine-drunk, to Beowulf.

He himself had lost his glory and courage-fame

because he never dared

risk his life nor do brave deeds

with Hrunting or any other blade

under the waves' strife.

But now

he had prepared Beowulf for such a battle.

Beowulf spoke, son of Ecgtheow:

    "I am glad, eager for this battle!

    Glorious son of Halfdane,

    gold-friend of man,

    remember what we said earlier:

    if in your service

    I should yield up my life,

    then you would ever be in my father's place.

    If this battle takes me,

    protect my young kin-thanes,

    my hand-chosen war-band.

    Beloved Hrothgar,

    all the treasures you gave me

    send on to Hygelac, son of Hrethel.

    When he stares on the gold-gleaming treasure,

    may that Geats' lord see

    that I found a good king,

    a generous ring-giver,

    and lived well while I served him.

    Unferth, I give you

    my wondrous wave-bladed sword,

    an ancient heirloom

    whose hard-edges are widely-known to men.

    I will take your blade, Hrunting,

    and gain glory or taste death."

Without waiting for an answer,

the prince of the Weder-Geats

ran to the banks of the mere

and the lake-surge took him under.

Much of the day passed

before Beowulf at last reached lake-bottom.

The grim and greedy she-creature

who had ruled the water-mere ravenously,

fiercely, for one-hundred seasons,

saw one of the humans from above

had come down to her monster-realm.

She laid hold of the warrior,

seized him in her poison claws,

but her loathsome fingers failed to impale him,

for his battle-sark,

hand-locked iron ring-mail,

protected his bone-hoard.

The lake-wolf bore the rings' chieftain

through gore-water to her court,

and in her grasp, no matter how bold he was,

he could wield no weapons.

Deep-down through the waves

many monsters assailed him,

sea-beasts

tore at his sark with battle-tusks

and harried him with horrors.

Soon the hero was in a hostile hall

where there was no water,

because the cavern-roof

kept out the mere-flood.

He saw firelight clearly blazing,

brightly shining.

With his full force,

he attacked the water-wolf,

the mighty mere-woman

and swung his battle-blade at her head.

The ring-sword

screamed a greedy war-song,

but Beowulf

discovered the blade would neither bite

nor scathe her life.

The bright edge failed the noble at need.

Though it had endured many hand-clashes,

sheared many helms,

broken through doomed mens' battle-dress,

this was the first time

the bright glory of the famed treasure

had faded.

Once again, Hygelac's kinsman,

mindful of glories,

was not slow in courage.

He threw the wave-marked sword to the earth

where it lay strong and iron-edged.

He cared not for his life,

but trusted in his own strength,

his great hand-grip.

So shall a man do when he is in battle

and hopes to gain long-lasting praise.

 In full fury, the Geats' leader

 seized Grendel's mother by the shoulder

and threw her to the floor.

She quickly clasped him against her

with a grim grip.

The weary-minded warrior,

strongest foot-fighter,

stumbled then, and he fell.

She bestrode her unwelcome hall-guest

and drew her broad, bright-edged dagger.

Now she would avenge her son,

her only off-spring.

Beowulf's braided breast-net

protected him from point and edge,

withstood her attack.

If not for that war-byrnie, hardest battle-net,

the Geats' champion, son of Ecgtheow,

would have perished.

But Fate granted him favor once more.

When he leaped up

he saw among the armor

a victory-blessed blade,

a sturdy-edged old-sword.

It was a warrior's honor,

the choicest handiwork of giants,

a beautiful war-weapon,

the best,

but it was bigger

than any other man could bear

into battle-play.

Beowulf, Scylding champion,

bristling and battle-grim,

seized the hilt and swung the ring-sword.

That blade bit sharply through her neck.

Bone-rings broke

as the blade

ran through her cursed flesh-cloak

and she sank to the floor,

bathed in sword-sweat.

Beowulf rejoiced in his hand-work.

All around him,

the cavern gleamed with gold,

glimmered like the sky candle

brightly shining.

He swiftly raised his weapon hard by the hilt

and looked toward the wall

where he saw Grendel,

lying on a bed life-less, battle-beaten,

put to death by Beowulf's hard hand-grip

on that fiend's last raid in Heorot.

Once more

Beowulf stood fierce and full of purpose.

More than once

this shadow-walker

had slain Hrothgar's kin-thanes

in slumber,

devoured sleeping Danes

in hateful sport

and Beowulf yearned

to repay Grendel for his many crimes.

Hrunting's edge

would not be useless now.

Beowulf cut off Grendel's head,

repaying the fiend

with one brutal sword-stroke,

a corpse-splitter.

Beside the mere-bank

Hrothgar and his men kept watch.

They saw the wave-swirl

stir up blood-streaked water,

and Hrothgar's men,

gathered about the gray-maned ring-giver,

said the victory-proud Geat hero

would not return to seek the glorious ruler,

said the sea-wolf had destroyed him.

Sorrowing, Hrothgar and his Scyldings

departed from thence to Heorot.

The Geat war-band sat downcast and heart-sick,

staring at the mere.

They wished, but did not expect,

to see their friend-lord again.

Under the water, the giant-made war-blade

waned in deadly icicles, a wonder great.

Blood dripped down like winter's water-ropes

when frost's bonds yield to spring

in the march of the seasons.

The wave-streaked slaughter-sword melted

in the poisonous blood of the sea-wolf

who had yielded up her life days in her cavern.

Though he saw heaped treasures in the hall

all around him,

Beowulf took nothing more than Grendel's head

and the hilt of the giant's sword

that had perished in the hot battle-sweat

of the poisonous fiend

who had died in her cavern.

He who had survived the fight

began swimming up through the wave-surges,

cleansed when the mere-monster

gave up the day-count of her loaned life.

Beowulf, sea-men's leader

and stout-hearted swimmer, came to land.

He greeted his men and rejoiced in his sea-loot,

the mighty burdens

which he carried with him.

The joyous war-band

gave throat in gladness that he was safe.

Helm and byrnie

were quickly loosed

from the favored hero.

Beside them, the mere now slept,

its water blood-flecked under the gray clouds.

With happy hearts

they fared forth by foot-tracks and earthways,

paced the known roads.

The king-bold men, stout-hearted,

carried the head from the lake-cliff,

an arduous task for the four soldiers

who carried Grendel's head on spear-shafts

to the gold-hall.

Soon, fourteen Geats, bold war-keen men,

came marching along the mead-path

and into Heorot.

In their midst strode their thane-lord,

a deed-bold man worthy of glory,

a battle-brave hero

to gladly greet Hrothgar.

Grendel's head was borne by its mane

onto the floor where men were drinking,

a sight

that filled the earls and the women

with awe.

All stared at the hideous spectacle.

Beowulf spoke, son of Ecgtheow:

> "Harken, son of Halfdane,
>
> lord of the Scyldings!
>
> We Geats have gladly
>
> brought you these sea-spoils,
>
> glory's tokens, which you see here.
>
> I risked war under water with much hardship.
>
> The deed was difficult, for
>
> I could not gain victory with Hrunting,
>
> though the weapon is good.
>
> I would have fallen,
>
> but fate often favors the un-doomed man.
>
> To me was given the good luck
>
> to see an heirloom-sword on the wall.
>
> With that weapon
>
> I killed the cavern-dweller,
>
> the she-monster, in a hard fight.
>
> Then the serpent-waved blade of that sword
>
> burned up, bathed in her hottest battle-sweat.
>
> I have brought you back the sword-hilt,
>
> as is fitting,
>
> and have avenged the slaughter of Danes.
>
> I rid the world of the grim-hearted creature,
>
> guilty of murder, and his mother, too.
>
> Now, chieftain of the Scyldings,
>
> I promise that you
>
> and all your soldiers' company,

all your thanes,

the young men and veterans of your nation,

may sleep sorrowless in Heorot.

You need have no dread for your heroes

as you did before."

Into the lap of the aging man,

hoary battle-leader, the hilt was placed,

the ancient work of giants' wonder-smiths.

Thus, into the keeping of the world-kings

passed the finest hilt of those

who in Danish lands dealt treasures.

Hrothgar gazed long at the hilt of the old heirloom

—rune-staves cut into the golden hilt-shanks

told for whom the sword

had first been made of irons most excellent,

writhe-hilted and serpent-marked.

Then spoke the wise son of Halfdane

and all fell silent:

"It may truly be said by those

who accomplish truth and right among the folk,

remembering from days of old

those who kept the kingdom,

that this hero Beowulf,

battle-friend,

was born better.

Glory is raised up beyond wide ways,

good friend, over each of your nations.

Steadfastly keep it all,

strength with heart's wisdom.

I shall fulfil my oath of friendship

as we earlier agreed.

Your comfort to your nations

will be long-lasting, a help to your heroes.

Not so was Heremod

to the offspring

of Ecgwala of the Honor-Scyldings.

He did not become powerful for their pleasure,

but for death

and the slaughter of the Danish people.

He felled in fury-mood

his feast companions and close comrades.

In his heart

he harbored blood-thirsty breast-thoughts

and gave no glory-rings to the Danes.

Joyless he survived,

suffered lengthy affliction and pain.

Learn from that

and guard yourself against malice,

Beowulf beloved, best of warriors.

The loaned body declines,

fated to fall in the end.

Another inherits the hoard

who deals out treasure

and a hero's ancient wealth

without thinking,

heeds not the horror.

Choose better, famed champion!

Learn from me, wise in winters.

 Glory in your strength while you live,

 for in time

you may find that sickness or sword-edge

will strip you of your prowess

or fire's embrace,

or flood's surge,

or bite of blade,

or spear's flight

or horrid old-age

will dim and darken

the brightness of your eyes.

Suddenly, dear warrior,

death will overpower you.

Remember,

I ruled the Ring-Danes

for a hundred seasons under the sky.

I defended them with spears and swords

in wars from unnumbered enemies

upon this middle-earth.

But setback came

here in my homeland,

grief after gladness,

when the ancient enemy Grendel

became my invader.

I endlessly suffered

great grief from his attacks.

I give thanks to Odin

that I lived long enough

to see with my own eyes

Grendel's sword-bloodied head

after such ancient strife.

Dear war-honored soldier,

go now to the bench and take your mead-joy.

When morning comes,

   we will share many treasures."

The glad-hearted Geat went at once

to seek the bench as the wise king ordered.

Then as before, a fine feast was prepared

for bold warriors and hall sitters

a second time.

Night-helm grew dim

and dark descended over the host in Heorot.

The aged Scylding, gray-maned king,

wished then his bed to seek.

The Geat hero also, famed shield-fighter,

desired rest, suddenly weary.

Beowulf, hall-thane from the far country,

led here by Fate,

had gladly attended all his thane's needs,

as all warrior-sailors

are duty-bound to do.

The open-hearted man rested then,

as the hall towered, silent and peaceful,

gabled and gold-gleaming.

The honored guest slept within

until black ravens, heaven's joy,

greeted the day glad-hearted.

Then came

the bright hurrying shine against shadow

and the warriors hastened,

noble ones full of eagerness

to fare back home.

They wished to seek their brave-spirited ship.

Beowulf told Unferth, son of Eclaf,

to take back his sword

and bear Hrunting well,

thanked him for the loan

of the beloved iron,

a worthy war-friend.

He did not defame the sword's edge,

or remind Unferth it had failed at need,

for Unferth was a proud man.

And then, journey-eager,

the warriors stood armored and ready.

Beowulf, dear to the Danes,

sought the high seat,

and the battle-bold hero greeted Hrothgar:

> "Now we sea-farers,
>
> come from a far country,
>
> say we are eager to return to Hygelac.
>
> You have entertained us worthily
>
> and we were well-treated.
>
> If there is anything on earth
>
> I can do more to earn your heart's love,
>
> dear warrior's lord,
>
> than I yet did with war-deeds,
>
> I am ready at once to do your bidding.
>
> If, over the flood's expanse,
>
> I hear that your neighbor-tribes

threaten you with terror as they once did,

I will bring a thousand thanes,

heroes to help.

I know my folk-guardian, lord Hygelac,

though young,

will support me with words and actions

and I will honor you with

spear-shafts and strong forces

whenever you need men.

If your son, Hrethric, decides

to come to the courts of the Geats,

he will find many friends there—

far countries are better sought

by one who himself is strong."

Hrothgar spoke:

"Your words, loved-lord,

were spoken to my heart.

I have not heard a man

of so young an age

speak with more wisdom.

You are strong in power

and knowing in heart,

a wise word-speaker.

I deem that if it comes about

that the spear takes

Hygelac, battle-fierce Hrethel's heir,

or if he falls to disease or iron

and you still live,

the Sea-Geats

could not choose a finer king

or hoard-guard of heroes

if you rule the kingdom.

Your mind-heart well pleases me,

dear Beowulf.

You have gained peace

for the Geats and for the Spear-Danes.

Now strifes and hostilities

which they endured in past years

will subside,

and while I wield this wide kingdom,

treasures shall be shared.

Many men will greet others

with good gifts over the gannet's bath.

Ring-prows will bring gifts

and peace-tokens over the ocean.

I now know the Geat people

as both foe and friend,

and am firmly prepared

to hold them entirely faultless

and without blame."

In the hall, the son of Halfdane,

earl's protector,

gave to Beowulf twelve treasures

and wished him a safe and swift return

to his loved land.

Then the Scylding chief and noble king

kissed the battle-bold warrior

and embraced him.

Beowulf was so dear to him

Hrothgar could not hold back

his breast-surge,

and released his tear-flood.

In his old wise-mind

lived two thoughts, one stronger:

that they would never meet again,

brave in counsel.

The other,

firmly fixed by thought-bonds in his heart,

was that he wished this noble man

for his own son.

Then went Beowulf,

gold-proud war-man

triumphant in treasure,

to tread the grass-mold path

toward the sea-walker

awaiting its owner-lord

on the wave's edge.

Onto the sandy-shore

strode the young-warriors' band,

full hearted, wearing ring-mail

and linked battle-sarks.

The land-guard saw the heroes' return

as he had before,

but this time

he did not greet them with scorn

from the cliff's height.

He rode to meet them,

welcomed the Wederas' people,

as the bright-armored

fighters fared to their ship.

They loaded the empty ring-prow,

wave-curved ship,

with war-clothes, treasures, and horses.

The mast of tallest timber

towered over Hrothgar's hoard-wealth.

Beowulf gave a bound-gold sword

to the boat-guard,

so that ever after on the mead-bench,

he was made worthier by that heirloom.

Then the ship put out to deep water

and left the Dane-lands behind.

On the journey home,

Hrothgar's gift-giving was often praised.

They said this was one king

entirely faultless, until age

took away his strength's joys,

which for many is their undoing.

They fastened a mighty sea-sheet

onto the mast with rope.

The sea-beam boomed;

wealthy wind-billows

could not hold back the wave-cleaver;

foamy-necked she fared forth,

fast over the swells.

The prow flew over the ocean's streams

until they saw the Geats' cliffs

and well-known headlands

Then the wind-driven keel surged up

and stood once more

on the long-desired land.

The Geat-land's harbor-guard

who had long watched the waves

and gazed far out to sea,

saw at last the loved ship-men

returning home on the eager current.

He ran to meet the sea-warriors

at the water's edge.

The broad-bosomed boat

was swiftly roped to land

with firm anchor-bonds

lest the waves' force

break apart the well-worked timbers.

Beowulf ordered the battle-won treasure-hoard

borne ashore,

all the jewels and plated gold

and battle-bright weapons.

The wealth's wielder,

Hygelac, Hrethel's son,

dwelt near-by with his war-band,

close by the sea-wall.

The bold-famed king

lived in a bright mead-hall

with Hygd, his wife, Hareth's daughter.

Though she was young

and had not lived many winters with him,

she was wise and well-honored

was not overly-humble nor bent down by life,

nor was she grudging of giving good gifts

of hoard-wealth to the Geats' people.

Hygd was un-like Modthryth,

now a fine folk-queen,

who had once committed fearful crimes.

No hall-thane but the great earl himself

dared to look into her eyes.

If a man returned her gaze he was seized,

tied in hand-woven bonds,

and his doom decided

when the serpent-bladed sword

sang his slaughter-song.

It is not a good custom for a woman,

queen or peace-weaver,

to deprive a loved man of his life

following an insult from her own mind.

However, Hemming's kinsman

put an end to that.

The ale-drinkers said

after her father gave Modthryth,

adorned in gold, to Offa,

young warrior of noble lineage,

she fared to his hall in a voyage

over the fallow flood.

After that,

she practiced harm and hatred much less,

gained fame for her goodness on that throne,

and enjoyed her life's destiny.

 She held great love for Offa, the heroes' lord

—by my knowledge the finest of all men

between the seas—

because in battles and gift-giving

he was a brave spear-man,

widely honored,

a wise-ruler of his homeland.

To him, Eomer was born,

a help to heroes and strong in battle.

He was Hemming's kinsman,

grandson of Garmund.

Then went Beowulf, hardy warrior,

over the sea-plain's wide foreshores

along the sand

with his hand-picked troop.

The world-candle

shone eager-bright from the south.

Their return journey was ended

and they swiftly marched to the stronghold

where within sat Hygelac, heroes' shield,

young battle-king and slayer of Ongentheow.

They had heard he was good at dealing out rings.

Beowulf's approach was quickly reported.

The warriors' defender and shield-companion

had returned to the homestead alive,

un-harmed from battle-play,

and was nearing the hall.

The mighty king ordered the floor cleared

for foot-guests.

After the ring-lord greeted the loyal thane

with formal speech and heart-filled words,

he who had survived the fight sat down with him,

kinsman to kinsman, nephew and uncle.

Hareth's daughter

passed through the hall with mead cups,

and carried drinking horns

to the heroes' hands.

Hygelac began to question his loved thane

from the high seat,

urged by his curiosity

to learn about the Sea-Geats' adventures.

He asked,

 "How fared you on your journey,

  dear Beowulf,

  when you suddenly decided to seek battle

far over the salt water

and do combat in Heorot?

Were you able to amend

Hrothgar's wide-known woe?

I seethed in floods of sorrow,

not sure my beloved man would return.

I long begged you to let the South-Danes

settle their war with Grendel themselves.

But now to Odin I give thanks

that I see you again, sound, and safe."

Beowulf, son of Ecgtheow, spoke:

"Lord Hygelac, what happened in Denmark

in the mighty struggle

between me and Grendel

is known to many men.

That fiend caused

too many sorrows and long misery

for the Spear-Danes,

but I avenged it all.

Grendel's kinsmen

have no need to boast upon the earth,

for those loathed wights

won no glory

from the dawn-clash between us.

When I first went to Heorot, Hrothgar's ring-hall,

the famed son of Halfdane

welcomed my heart-thoughts

and seated me with his own sons.

The Dane-king's shield-men were content.

I have never in all my life seen hall-sitters

under heaven's hollow

who have more mead-joy.

Wealhtheow, his famed queen,

peace-pledge of the people,

passed through the hall

and made young warriors bold.

Often she would give bits of twisted gold

or gold-rings to the soldiers

before she went to sit beside her lord.

Freawaru, daughter of Hrothgar,

bore unending ale-horns

to the hall-sitters,

many of whom she called by name

as she handed jeweled cups

to all the heroes.

Her father, the wise Scylding lord

and keeper of the kingdom,

has promised her,

gleaming with gold,

to Ingeld, glad son of Froda,

reckoning her as a peace-weaver

who will settle many blood feuds and conflicts.

But when a leader falls,

very seldom does the deadly

spear lie idle for long,

though the bride is good.

It may yet anger the chief of the Heatho-bards

and all his thanes

when Ingeld walks to the floor with Freawaru,

and all men see that her retainers,

Dane-mens' sons,

hard and ring-adorned,

are feasted while

glistening with twisted-gold heirlooms,

treasures from their own lost hoard.

Though they were able

to wield their weapons in the shield-play

they destroyed dear companions

and their own lives.

Who could guess the sorrow if an old warrior

speaks out at the beer feast,

one who sees a sword

and remembers the spear-death

of the soldiers?

The old fighter has a fierce heart

and he begins, sad-minded,

to test some young warrior's courage,

hoping to waken war-ruin with these words:

'Do you recognize that sword, my friend,

that precious iron-edge?

Under his war mask,

your own father carried it into battle

on his last campaign,

but he was slain by Danes

who ruled the slaughter-field

when Withergild

lay dead after the heroes' fall.

Look well!

There stands one of those slayers,

someone's son, exultant in his finery,

walking on the hall-floor

and boasting of murder.

He is wearing that heirloom-treasure
which you by right should possess.'
Such a one urges thus and reminds often
with his bitter words
until the time comes
that Freawaru's thane,
blade-bitten and blood-stained
sleeps, forfeits his life
for his father's deeds.
The other, who knows the region well,
escapes alive.
Then on both sides
earls' sworn oaths will be broken
and slaughter-hate will surge in Ingeld.
After the first-flood of care,
wife-love becomes cooler.
I do not think the Heatho-Bards' loyalty
is un-treacherous for the Danes,
nor is their friendship firm.
Now I shall speak again of Grendel,
so that you may know well,
treasure-giver mine,
what happened
in the hand-clash of heroes.

After heaven's gem
had glided over the earth
the angry guest came,
terrible and evening-grim,
to seek us
where we guarded the hall unharmed.

For Hondscio, girded-Geat fighter,

the battle was fatal.

Death-doomed, he was the first fated to fall.

Grendel was to him the mouth-slayer,

and devoured

the beloved man's body—all of it.

Then the empty-handed fiend

wanted to leave the gold hall,

bloody-toothed and slaughter-mad,

but he grasped me with his greedy hand

and wished to test my strength.

On his body, Grendel bore a glove,

huge and strongly crafted,

secured with clasps

and skillfully made from dragon-skins.

He wanted to stuff me inside it,

but I fiercely fought against him

and he could not.

It will take too long to tell

how I paid requital

to that folk-scourge for all his evils.

I honored you, my chief,

and your people,

by my acts.

Grendel pulled away from me,

thinking to escape,

but left behind

his arm,

which I hung beneath the eaves of Heorot.

He ran to the mere-ground,

wretched and gloomy-hearted,

and sank to the depths.

After the death-clash,

when morning came,

and we sat down to feast,

the Scylding lord rewarded me

with plated gold and many treasures.

There was song and merriment.

Hrothgar, the old Scylding,

is steeped in learning

and told stories from long ago.

Sometimes a warrior

would strum the glee-wood for pleasure,

sometimes sing a song, true and tragic.

Sometimes the open-hearted king

would recite word-for-word

some strange tales.

Sometimes,

the age-knotted ancient warrior

would lament his youth and battle-strength.

His heart welled up within

when he, wise in winters,

remembered much.

So we took our pleasure

the whole long day

until night came, another to men.

Then was Grendel's mother

ready for grief-revenge, and set out

full of sorrow from her lair.

Death had snatched her son,

who was full of war-hate

for the Wederas.

The monster-woman avenged her child
by savagely killing Aeschere,
the king's most loved warrior.
When morning came,
the Danes could neither burn
nor place the beloved man on the bale-fire
because the she-wolf,
in her fiendish embrace,
had carried off the corpse
under the mountain stream.
That was the bitterest sorrow
suffered by Hrothgar, the Scylding lord,
in Grendel's long siege.
Then, by your life,
the king implored me in anguish
to risk my life in the water's rush
and gain more glory
for which he promised more rewards.
So, as is widely known,
I found the mere's
grim and ghastly depth-guard.
For a while we were locked hand in hand,
and water welled with gore
until I cut off the head
of Grendel's mother with a giant's sword
I found in her war-hall.
Fate freed me from death-doom once more,
and the son of Halfdane
again handed me many treasures.
That tribe-king lived honorably,
and I by no means

passed up his gifts,

great rewards for my strength.

Hrothgar gave me treasures

I chose for my own.

So now, my loved kin-lord, these gifts

I wish to graciously offer to you.

All favor depends upon you,

dear Hygelac,

for few other close kinsmen do I have."

Then Beowulf ordered his war-band

to bring in the boar-crested standard,

battle-steep helmet, gray byrnie,

the glorious war-sword,

and took up the tale again:

"Hrothgar gave me this battle gear,

and ordered that with some words

I should first

tell you of its ancestry:

long had it belonged to Heorogar,

leader-king of the Scyldings,

and at his death,

the breast armor went to bold Heoroweard,

who was loyal to him. Use it all well."

I have heard that with the treasures,

four horses, apple-yellow and all alike,

followed behind.

Beowulf offered all the gifts to Hygelac.

So shall kinsmen act,

and not weave malice-nets for others

with secret cunning,

or contrive death for close companions.

To Hygelac, the battle-fierce warrior-king,

Beowulf, his nephew, was very loyal,

and each kept the other's favor well in mind.

I have also heard that the exquisite neck-gem

Wealhtheow had given Beowulf,

he presented to Hygd along with three horses,

supple and saddle-bright.

Hygd accepted all,

and joyfully adorned her breast

with that wonder-jewel.

Thus Beowulf, son of Ecgtheow,

showed boldness.

The man famed for combat

and for good deeds

had acted in pursuit of honor.

He never, when drunk,

slew his hearth-thanes.

He did not have a cruel heart.

He treasured the generous gift

of mankind's greatest strength,

Fate's battle-brave blessing.

In his home-fort,

Beowulf had long been thought lowly.

The Geats' sons had never sung of him

on the mead-benches,

nor had the lord of the Wederas

given him much honor.

It had been strongly thought

that Beowulf was lazy,

careless in his youth.

But turn-about had come

to the glory-favored man

for these past mis-thinkings.

Hygelac, heroes' keeper,

ordered Hrethel's gold-gleaming heirloom

to be brought in

—among the Geats

there was no finer sword-shaped treasure

than this—

and he laid it in Beowulf's lap.

Hygelac also gave his nephew

seven-thousand hides of land,

a hall, and a high-seat.

The land had been theirs together

through inheritance,

though the broad kingdom belonged

to only one alone,

 Hygelac, who had been born a lord.

But in time, in battle-clashes of later days,

the broad kingdom passed into Beowulf's hands

when Hygelac lay dead

and Heardred fell in the shield-wall

after hard war-fighters

attacked the nephew of Hereric.

For fifty winters, Beowulf ruled the realm,

a wise king and aging land-warden,

until in dark nights a dragon began to rule,

who on the high-heath

guarded a hoard in a steep stone-barrow.

No man knew the path to that place.

But Fate led an unlucky runaway slave

to the path

and he fell into the barrow

where he saw the hoard

and its hideous keeper sleeping.

Seized by fear, he reached out his hand,

picked up a jeweled cup, and fled,

running back the way he had come.

The thief had not set out to seek the hoard

but to find refuge

from fierce beatings at his lord's hands,

storms of hate-blows for crime-guilt.

When he came upon the trove

and its terrible guard

he took the precious cup

as a chance to buy back his lord's favor.

There were many such ancient treasures

in the earth-house,

a huge hoard-legacy

from yore-days,

hidden there by a wise-thinking one

of noble kin.

Death took him and all his company

in former days,

and the last longest-living man,

friend-grieving,

expected the same fate.

He watched for death,

knowing there was little time

to enjoy the gold.

Under the sea-cliffs stood a barrow

near the wave-strife,

narrowly crafted into the gray rock walls

with cunning skill.

This last survivor, a loyal thane,

carried into the earth-house

his vanished lord's treasures,

all the hoard-worthy plated gold and heirlooms,

and spoke a few words:

    "Earth, the gold was taken from you

    by good men long ago,

    and after they had seen

    much hall-joy,

    war-death and life-murder

    took them each away.

    Now I have none who might wield sword

or polish the precious drink-cup,

for all have passed into Fate's keeping.

The hard helmet, adorned with gold,

shall be stripped of ornaments,

and those

who should burnish the battle-masks

now slumber.

War-mail, which in the shield-crash

felt the bite of iron,

decays like its lost warriors.

Byrnies ring no more

nor widely fare with war-fighters

in the heroes'-band.

There is no sound of glee-wood,

harp's delight,

nor does the good hawk

swoop through the hall.

No longer do we hear the swift stamp

of saddled horse in the door-yard,

for baleful death

has sent forth my kinsmen.

I return the gold to you, earth,

to hold once again,

for all our heroes are gone!"

So mourned the survivor, full of sorrow,

the last of his people.

Un-happy, he passed many long days and nights

until death's surge stilled his heart.

Thus the dragon, old dawn-destroyer

greatly dreaded by land dwellers,

found the gold-hoard

unguarded and standing open.

The naked foe-dragon,

night-flier enfolded in flame

and wise in serpent-ways,

he who must seek out barrows in the earth,

found his hoard-joy.

For such a one

there could be no better shelter.

Three-hundred winters the terrible tribe-smasher,

mighty and strong,

guarded the earth-hoard

until that unlucky wanderer

stirred the anger-embers in his dragon-heart.

The thief bore the stolen treasure to his king,

begged for a truce-pact,

and offered his lord

the hoard-plundered cup.

His ruler gazed for the first time

on the ancient work

and readily granted the wretched hoard-thief

his pardon.

But now the dragon

was awake, his war-need renewed.

Slithering over the stones

the strong-heart found his foe's footprint.

The cunning thief had stepped too near

the sleeping serpent's head.

Yet, Fate protected the undoomed thief

for a little while.

Now, eagerly, the hoard-keeper

searched over the open ground,

wished to find the man

who had treated him

so sorely while he slept.

Hot and fierce-hearted

he circled the barrow-mound ever outward

but could find no one in the wasteland,

yet he rejoiced in war, in battle's action.

 At times he returned to his barrow,

still seeking the cup,

and soon he knew that one man alone

had disturbed the gold,

the noble's treasure.

The hoard-guard waited impatiently

until evening came,

wishing to repay the foe for his theft

of the gleaming cup.

At last, to the worm's delight, the day vanished,

and in his barrow he would wait no longer.

He fared forth in rage and flame,

impelled by fire.

His attack was terrible,

and soon all Geat-land knew

of the fire-dragon's wrath.

The night-flier spewed flames

and burned bright homes.

To men's horror, the blaze-light spread.

The evil air-foe would leave nothing alive.

The cruel malice of the worm's war-strength

was widely seen from near and far,

and all could see how the death-bringer

aimed his harm and hatred at the Geat-folk.

In the pale darkness before dawn,

the dragon hurried back to his hidden hoard.

He had enfolded the land-dwellers

in flame and a burning blaze,

and now he trusted in his

hidden barrow's wall

and battle-strength to keep him secure.

But his trust would be tested.

Then Beowulf understood terror,

quickly and truly

for his own home, the finest

of buildings, the gift-seat of the Geats,

had melted in the burn-swells.

That was the deepest heart-misery

to the good man,

the greatest of mind-sorrows.

The aged ruler began to think

he had angered Odin,

and his breast welled with dark thoughts,

which was not usual for him.

The beloved old-ruler must now face

the end of his loaned-days,

his world-life;

the serpent, too, though he had lived long

upon the hidden hoard-wealth.

Beowulf, the war-king, the Wederas' chief,

devised revenge

for the dragon's fiery destruction

of the folks' fortress,

strong-hold of the coastal lands.

He, the earls' over-lord,

ordered the smiths to make him

a wondrous war-shield, all-iron,

a true warrior's protector,

for he knew well that tree-wood,

even the best linden boards,

could not help against fire.

Beowulf scorned to attack the flame-foe

with a large force, a full troop.

He did not fear the strife for himself

and he had no fear of the serpent's power,

strength, or courage,

for he had already survived

many daring perils, hostilities,

and battle-clashes in the long years

since he had purged Hrothgar's hall

of Grendel and his loathsome kin.

Not the least of those wars

was the battle in Frisia

when his lord Hygelac—

the Geats' war-king and folk-friend,

Hrethel's heir—was slain.

He died in sword-drink,

beaten down by blades in the shield wall.

From that war, Beowulf, by his own strength,

achieved his second swim-feat—

he plunged into the sea

bearing the battle-trappings of thirty earls.

The Hetware

have no need to exult against the Geats

over that foot-fight or those who bore shields

against them,

for few went back home to tell the tale.

Beowulf, son of Ecgtheow, wretched solitary survivor,

swam back to his tribe over the sea.

There, Hygd offered him wealth and the kingdom,

rings and the royal seat.

She thought her own son too young

to hold the native thrones against foreign armies

now that Hygelac was dead.

Beowulf, noble man,

said he would not be lord over Heardred,

would not choose to rule the kingdom,

but would trust in the young king.

So he continued to live among the folk.

He upheld friendly counsel

and gained the peoples' favor.

But in time, Ohthere, the king of the Swedes,

died, and his brother Onela,

son of Ongentheow, took the throne.

Ohthere's two sons rebelled against Onela

and became exile-men,

sought refuge with Heardred.

Onela attacked the Geats

for taking in the exiles,

and Heardred, for his hospitality,

received his death-wound by sword-strokes.

When Heardred lay dead,

Onela sailed back to Sweden

leaving Beowulf to rule the Geats.

That was a good king.

But Beowulf remembered his fallen chief

and planned revenge.

He became friend to Ohthere's son,

Eadgil, living in misery,

and supported him with his army of Geats,

and accompanied him over the wave-road

with warriors and weapons.

In cold grief-forays, Eadgil took his revenge

and deprived Onela of life.

Thus had Beowulf, son of Ecgtheow,

survived all enmities and cruel conflicts

with courage-deeds,

until the day came

when he must struggle with the serpent.

The anger-filled lord of the Geats

chose eleven from his army

and went to face the dragon.

Beowulf had since heard

from whence came the dragon's anger

and fierce hatred of men.

The cup had gone from thief to lord,

from lord to Beowulf, who now made

the cup-thief the thirteenth man

in his hand-chosen war-band.

The un-happy captive, heart-heavy,

who had brought the onset of the terror,

must now lead Beowulf's band to the barrow.

Against his will,

the thief led them to the earth-hall,

a place he alone knew,

the underground barrow

near the sea-surge and wave-strife.

Inside the earth-hall

full of jewels and golden wires

waited a terrible warden,

a wary war-fighter

who guarded the gold,

old under the earth.

This was not an easy bargain

for any man to gain.

Then the fight-hard king,

gold friend to the Geats,

stepped onto the headland

and wished his hearth-companions good luck.

Beowulf was restless,

sad-hearted, and slaughter-keen.

His doom had drawn too near

and the old man knew he must meet it,

must seek Fate's decision

to sever asunder life from his limbs.

He would not be wrapped in flesh much longer.

Beowulf, son of Ecgtheow, spoke:

> "In youth I survived
> many war-storms and battle-times.
> I remember it all.
> In my seventh winter, my treasure-prince,
> lord-friend of the people,
> took me from my father.
> Hrethel-king held me and kept me,

gave me wealth and feasting and father-love,

mindful of our kinship.

As a warrior in his stronghold,

he loved me no less than he did his own sons,

my kind uncle-friends

Herebeald and Hæthcyn

and my lord Hygelac.

Hrethel suffered un-looked for misery

when Hæthcyn bent his horn-bow,

missed his mark and struck down Herebeald

with a bloody bolt, one brother the other.

There could be no vengeance

for the fall of that prince

lest the father murder his remaining son.

So Hrethel suffers,

utters dirges and sorrowing songs,

like any father

whose young son rides the gallows in guilt,

hangs for ravens to relish,

and the father can neither avenge him

or provide any other help.

Each morning that father remembers

his son's death-day with an aching heart.

In his son's empty house

he sees a wasted wine-hall,

a wind-swept refuge bereft of joy;

the riders and heroes asleep in graves.

There is no sound of harp

or laughing on the benches

as there once was.

So that grieving father seeks his bed,

singing sorrow-dirges for himself

and for his dead son.

In his grief, Hrethel finds

the fields and dwelling places boundless,

too empty.

The Wederas' leader

suffers sorrow-surges for Herebeald,

but for Haethcyn the kin-slayer,

he feels neither

hate nor love.

So Hrethel gave up men's joys

and fared into Fate's keeping.

To his heirs he left land and a fortress,

as a good king should.

After Hrethel died, Swedes and Geats

shared battle-rage and terrible hostility

and met across the water in a fierce struggle.

Ongentheow's heirs were bold

with war-need

and would not hold the peace

across the waters.

Around Hreosnabeorh, where many fell,

they committed dreadful savage slaughter.

My kin-friends avenged that fiery feud

—as it has been told—

though Haethcyn paid with his life

for the conflict.

I heard that Ongentheow attacked Eofor

in revenge,

one kinsman the other,

with his sword-blade,

and split the old man's war-helm.
Ongentheow, the aged Scylfing,
fell, corpse-pale.
His old hands remembered many feuds
where he had not withheld the death-stroke.
I repaid Hygelac for the treasures he gave me
with my battle-prowess and shining sword
and he rewarded me with grants of land,
pieces of earth,
the joy of ownership of hearth and hall.
He had no need to seek among the Spear-Danes,
the Gifthas, or in the Swede's kingdom
for a worse war-fighter
or buy any with his wealth.
I stood alone in the vanguard,
leading the troop,
and thus shall I always act in battle
as long as this sword lasts,
like it always has
since the battle where I became
hand-slayer to Dayraven,
the Franks' champion.
Thus was that one
unable to bring to the Frisian king
the breast adornments and spoils of war.
He was a noble,
and their courageous banner-bearer.
It was not the blade that killed him,
but my battle-grip
which broke his bone-house
and stilled his heart-surges.

But now my hand

with this hard sword and blade's edge

must contend for the hoard."

Beowulf uttered his last boast-words:

"In my youth I tested my strength

and battle-wisdom many times.

Now as a wise folk-guardian

I welcome this feud.

If the worm attacks me from his ground-hall,

I shall win glory."

For the last time,

he spoke to each man in his war-band,

his bold helm-bearers and close companions:

"I would not bear weapons against this serpent

if I knew how else I might grapple for glory,

as I did with Grendel.

But here I expect the heat of battle-fire,

breath and poison,

therefore I will keep my shield and byrnie.

I will not flee

one foot's pace from the barrow's guard,

but at the wall we shall see

what Fate allots us.

I am so firm in mind that I will forebear

from boasting against the war-flier.

Remain by the barrow in your bright byrnies,

warriors in war-gear,

to see which of us

better survives the wounds

of the death-clash.

This is not your fight,

nor is it for you to wield your war-power here.

This peril is mine alone—

I will pit my strength

against the monster as a mighty earl should,

and with my courage

I shall gain the gold

or be taken from you in terrible slaughter."

Then the bold warrior arose with his shield

and put his trust in his own strength,

strong in his sword-sark

and boar-crested helm,

and went to the stone walls.

Such is not the coward's way.

Beowulf, ungrudgingly good,

who had survived many struggles

and army-clashes,

saw in the cliff-wall a standing stone arch.

It was the barrow-door

with steam rushing out

like the brook's surge

but hot with deadly fire.

He could not stand near

the hoard-guard's flame-stream

for much time or endure its depth unburned.

Strong at heart and full of anger,

Beowulf roared

a clear-ringing battle-challenge

into the gray stone barrow.

When he heard the man's voice

the hoard-guard's hate rose up,

and the wyrm knew

the time to plead for peace was over.

Forth flew the monster's breath,

hot battle-smoke,

and the earth thundered.

Beowulf, outside the barrow door,

raised his shield-face

toward the worm-flames.

Though each death-minded foe

was filled with dread toward the other,

the war-king and the ring-coiled dragon

were eager to meet the strife.

The war-king drew his sword,

an ancient heirloom

with edges un-blunted.

Beowulf, stout-hearted,

stood firm in his armor and steep shield

while the serpent swiftly coiled together,

and then the flame-foe slithered forth,

a burning serpent hastening to his fate.

The iron shield, wielded for this first time,

protected Beowulf's life and limbs

for a lesser-while

than the famed chieftain sought,

though Fate had not

judged him the winner in this battle.

Beowulf swung his war-blade

and struck the ghastly-hued dragon

but the edge would not bite, bright on bone,

and would not pass through

the dragon-skin.

After that battle-stroke the barrow-guard,

in baleful mood,

spewed death-fire,

covered the ground with battle-flames.

Beowulf, the Geat's gold-friend,

did not boast of glory-victories that day,

for the iron edge, good from ages past,

a shining sword in every fight,

should not have failed.

It was no easy feat for the son of Ecgtheow

to relinquish this earth-plain

and dwell elsewhere,

as we all must

when we take leave of our loaned-days.

It was not long before the fierce enemies

clashed together again.

Heartened by the man's failed stroke,

the hoard-guardian swelled with breath a new time,

and cruelly enfolded in fire

him who once ruled a kingdom.

Beowulf's war-band
of faithful hand-companions and nobles' sons
did not rush to stand with their lord
in valor,
but began to slink off into the forest
to save their lives.
Among them
was one whose heart surged with sorrows
—kinship can never be altered
for him who thinks rightly.
Wiglaf was his name, Weohstan's son,
acclaimed shield-fighter
and kinsman of Aelfhere.
He saw his kin-lord suffering dragon-heat
under his war-mask
and remembered
the honor Beowulf once gave him
—gifts of the wealthy home-land
of the Waegmundings
with all its folk-rights,
as his father had owned—
and could not hold back his hand.
He seized his yellow-linden shield
and drew his ancient sword.
The blade had been
a legacy for Eanmund, son of Othere.
But with that self-same sword

Weohstan slew Eanmund,

a friendless exile,

in the shield-wall of war

and took away Eanmund's bright-gleaming helm,

ringed byrnie,

and old-sword of giant-make.

He brought them to Onela,

but Onela gave back the sword,

and the bright war-clothing

without speaking of the battle,

though Weohstan had slain

his own brother's son.

Weohstan held the riches,

blade and byrnie

for many seasons,

until his son could perform deeds

like his old father,

and when he left this life,

he left the riches and gifts of war-clothing

to Wiglaf, Beowulf's nephew.

Now, in the dragon-clash,

was the first time the young warrior

had engaged in battle's rush

with his noble lord,

and his war-mood did not melt,

nor his father's legacy fail him

as the serpent would soon see

when they met.

Wiglaf, sad in heart,

called out to his craven companions:

> "Remember that time in the mead-hall
>
> when we promised Beowulf,
>
> the lord who gave us this bright armor,
>
> that we would repay him
>
> with these hard helms
>
> and sharp swords when the need arose.
>
> So of his own will
>
> he chose us from his army
>
> for this death-journey.
>
> He gave me these treasures
>
> and considered us all worthy.
>
> He reckoned us
>
> to be good soldiers and bold helm-bearers.
>
> Our folk-lord intended
>
> to do this courage-deed alone
>
> because he has achieved more glories
>
> than other men,
>
> but I deem the day has come
>
> when our ring-giver
>
> needs the strength of good warriors.
>
> Let us go and help our battle-leader
>
> while he is beset by this fierce fire-terror.
>
> For my part, it is more fitting
>
> that dragon-fire embraces me
>
> with my gold-giver.
>
> It does not seem right that we bear our shields
>
> back home

unless first we fell the fiery foe
and defend the life of our lord-friend.
Of all the Geats
he should not suffer pain or sink in strife alone.
Sword and helm, byrnie and battle-shroud
shall all work together."

He waited, but no one returned.

So, Wiglaf, lone warrior,

turned and waded through the death-smoke

to protect his lord, and said to him:

"Dear Beowulf, long-ago in your youth
you said that as long as you had breath
in your body
you would not let glory fail!
Now be resolute in your bold deeds
and defend your life
with all your strength!
I will aid you."

The serpent coiled forth again

with glowing fire-floods,

seeking his foes, the hated humans.

Waves of flowing flames

burned Wiglaf's shield away.

His byrnie provided no protection

to the young spear-fighter,

so he sought shelter with Beowulf

under his iron shield.

From his main-strength,

Beowulf called forth his past glories

and struck at the dragon again,

so that his sword, driven by his mighty hand,

stuck fast in the serpent's head.

But Naegling, Beowulf's sword,

failed to kill the beast,

for fate had not granted

him the help of iron-edges in battle.

His hand was so strong that

—by my knowledge—

he over-strained

every blade he ever wielded,

every battle-hardened blade he bore.

No weapon ever did him any better

than the strength of his own hand.

Now for the third time,

the fierce fire-dragon, hot and battle-grim,

saw his chance and rushed the brave king.

He clamped Beowulf's neck

in his fiendish fangs

and drenched him

in blood and waves of gore.

Then, as I have heard,

Wiglaf, at Beowulf's side,

showed his courage,

the strength and boldness

that was his from birth.

He took no heed

of the serpent's head,

and though his hand was burned,

the brave hero came to his kin-lord's need.

He struck the hated foe lower down,

on its neck.

His sword sank in, gleaming and golden,

and the foe-fires began to slacken.

Beowulf, still the battle-chief

and in full command of his wits,

drew his bitter battle-dagger from his byrnie

and with his full strength

he sliced the serpent through its middle.

That was the last victory-feat for Beowulf

in the living world.

Both kin-nobles had battered the beast.

They felled the foe—their courage

claimed its life.

A man should be as Wiglaf,

a good thane at need.

Beowulf's wound, dealt by the earth-dragon,

began to sting and swell;

the poison in his breast

raged with deadly pain,

so the noble king

made his way to a seat in the wall

and with weary eyes,

looked on the work of giants,

the stone arches standing on firm pillars

and holding the worm's timeless earth-house

inside.

Wiglaf turned to his friend-lord

and loosed his helm.

With his sword-bloody hands

he washed the worm-wounds

of his battle-sated friend with water.

Beowulf had endured all of earth's joys

through his long day-count

and knew that

the tally of his years was finished.

Death drew near.

Beowulf spoke:

"If I had been given a son, an heir,

to him would I give these war-weeds, my armor.

I ruled the nation fifty winters.

None of our neighboring folk-kings

dared bring their warriors against me

or oppressed us with terrors.

I awaited Fate's decree,

kept my own counsel,

never sought treacheries,

nor swore any unjust oaths.

When these death-wounds

take my breath from my body

I can rejoice in my life,

because no one need blame me

for any baleful murder of kin.

Good Wiglaf, dear kin-thane,

now that the Worm lies

in sorely wounded sword-sleep,

bereft of treasure,

go quickly to where the hoard

sits beneath the gray stones

and look at it with a wise heart.

Hasten, Wiglaf,

so that I might see the old riches,

the gold-store,

and keenly gaze at the shining skill-gems,

so it might be easier to leave my life

and the nation which I long ruled."

After Beowulf's request, as I have heard,

Wiglaf, son of Weohstan

obeyed the battle-sick king.

In his war-stained ring-mail

and braided battle-sark

the young warrior went in

under the barrow's roof.

There was no sign of the serpent,

for their blades

had taken his life.

The victorious thane saw many rich jewels

and heaps of gold glittering on the ground,

wondrous hangings on the wall.

In the dragon's den

he saw the old shadow-flier's cups standing,

flagons of former days

now stripped of their ornaments,

their burnishers gone.

Many old and rusty helms gathered dust

beside long-cold arm-rings

of skillfully twisted gold.

Treasures, or gold in the ground,

may easily overwhelm any man,

hide it who will.

High over the hoard,

Wiglaf saw a golden standard

woven long ago with agile fingers' skill,

the greatest of hand-wonders.

It shone with a light so bright

he could gaze clearly

upon all the treasure at his feet.

Then it is said he plundered the hoard

one man in a treasure of old giants' work.

He chose bowls and plates

and carried them in his bosom.

He also pulled down the shining standard,

brightest of beacons.

The iron-edged blade of the ancient lord

had already wounded

the treasures' long-time protector,

he who waged fire-terror at midnights

 until he in slaughter died.

Wiglaf hurried, eager to return,

urged on by the treasure.

He wondered whether or not

his bold-hearted chieftain

would still be alive

in the blood-field

where he had left him.

He found Beowulf, glorious chief,

his own lord, bleeding and at life's end.

He sprinkled him with more water

until his lord's farewell words

pierced through his breast-hoard.

Old in grief,

the Warrior-king gazed at the gold and said:

"I thank Odin, father of all,

that I was able to store up such

glory for my people

before my death-day.

I have paid for the treasure-hoard

with my alotted life.

Wiglaf, see to the needs of our nation

from this day forth

for I no longer can.

Order my famed shield-fighters

to build a mound

on the ocean's cape,

and after my bale-fire is cold,

men shall know

it stands as a reminder to my people.

Towering high on Hronesness,

wave-warriors

and all who sail ships

over the misty seas from afar

will call it Beowulf's barrow."

The old king

took a golden chain from his neck

and gave it to Wiglaf.

"If I had been granted an heir of my body,

I would now give to my son these war-weeds."

So saying, he gave to the young spear-fighter

his gold-bright helm, ring-mail,

and byrnie,

and told him to use them well.

"You are the last of the Waegmundings,

the last of us all.

Fate has taken

our kinsmen to their destined death,

all the warriors in their strength.

I must go after them."

Beowulf spoke the last words

from his breast-hoard

before he went to

the fierce flames of his bale-fire

and his heart flew to seek his glory.

Wiglaf, young untried warrior,

grieved as he gazed at the dearest man

lying on the ground,

his lord-friend who had suffered

a wretched, painful death.

Beside him lay the terrible earth-dragon,

king-slayer, bereft of life,

balefully beaten down.

The coiled serpent

no longer kept the ring-hoard,

for iron-edges had taken away his life.

The hammer-forged swords

of two brave kinsmen

had left him lifeless on the slaughter-field.

The wide-flier had fallen near his hoard-cave,

stilled by his wounds.

He would fare no more

through midnight skies,

proud of his rich possessions

and bright flames,

for he was brought down

by the war-chief's handwork.

To my knowledge, there are few battle-men,

however brave or bold,

who would dare the fiery challenge

of a waking dragon,

and fewer still

who would steal treasure

from an earth-hoard

when they found its keeper

awake and watching.

Beowulf's death

paid for his share

of the princely treasure

when each of them,

serpent and king,

had reached the end

of their loaned lives.

Then the battle-slackers

came out of the forest,

ten together, timid trust-breakers

who had not dared

raise their ash-wood

in aid of their friend-lord's large need.

Ashamed, they walked

in their un-bloodied war-clothing,

dragging their shields

to where the old man lay.

By their lord's shoulder

sat the weary Wiglaf,

proud foot-fighter,

trying in vain to wake Beowulf with water.

Though he wished with all his strength

to bring life back to his chieftain,

he could not,

for no one can turn aside Odin's will—

he chooses the dead as he ever has.

Sore at heart, Wiglaf

stared long at the unloved warriors.

When he spoke, his grim rebuke
was easily heard by them all:
    "The loved-lord who gave you treasures
    and war-clothing
    —the grandest he could find far or near—
    who handed out helms and byrnies
    to you hall-thanes on his benches
    woefully wasted those gifts
    when he met his hour of greatest need.
    In no way could such a battle-king
    boast of you as war comrades,
    yet when Beowulf faced death alone,
    Odin granted him the victory
    and our thane-lord
    avenged this feud with his sword.
    When his moment of doom came,
    too few defenders thronged around our chief.
    I tried to help my kinsman
    beyond the measure of my strength
    and gave him what life-protection I could,
    but I am weaker than our ring-giver.
    I struck the serpent with my sword
    and his fierce flames slackened,
    they flew with less force from his head,
    but Beowulf delivered the death stroke.
    Now heed well my words:
    treasure-getting and sword-giving,
    all homeland joys for your kin
    shall cease.
    When nobles from afar learn of your flight

and inglorious deed

they will rush to attack

and bring war to our nation.

All of you, and your kin-clans,

will be deprived of land-rights.

Death is better for all men than a life of shame."

Wiglaf then commanded a messenger

to take the tale of the battle-deeds

to the Geats' camp up on the headlands.

The warrior-troop of hardy shield-bearers

had waited there since early morning,

expecting news of their lord's death-day

or the dear man's return.

The messenger held back no tidings

and said before all:

"The joy-giver of the Wederas' nation

the lord of the Geats,

lies in slaughter-rest from the serpent's deeds!

Beside him lies his life-taker,

sick with dagger-wounds.

In no way

could the sword deliver death

to the monster.

Wiglaf, son of Weohstan,

sits over Beowulf,

the living over the unliving,

holding heart-weary head-watch

over the loved and the loathed.

When the fall of our king

becomes widely known

to the Franks and the Frisians,
war-times will come for our nation.

This quarrel was shaped long-ago
when Hygelac fared with his sea-force
to the Frisians' land
and attacked the Hetware.
His mailed warriors
were met with over- powering strength
and he fell with his foot-troop.
He gained no rings or gold for his warriors
in that feud.
From that day forth,
the Merovingian king
has granted us no mercy,
nor do I expect peace or trust
from the Swede's tribe,
for it is widely known
that Ongentheow took the life of Hæthcyn,
Hrethel's son, at Ravenswood,
when he arrogantly attacked
the Geats' nation of War-Scylfings.
The wise father
of Ohthere returned the attack,
cut down the sea-leader,
and rescued his wife,
an aged woman,
mother to Ohthere and Onela,
though they lost her gold.
They pursued their enemies ruthlessly
until that troop escaped in Ravenswood

without a lord.
Ongentheow besieged the wretched remnant
with his vast army.
All through the night
he roared out to them
that when morning broke
he would slaughter them all
and hang their heroes from the trees
for the ravens' delight.
But instead, early day brought the sound
of Hygelac's war-horns to the war-weary band,
relief to their anguished minds.
That good king
brought his tribe's troop of thanes.
The gory track of Swedes and Geats
in the death-clash of men was widely seen,
and both armies kept the battle
strong between them.
But Ongentheow had long heard
of Hygelac's battle-skills and war-craft.
He didn't believe his sea-men
could withstand the Geat war-sailors
and defend the hoard
of children and women,
so he drew his armies back
behind an old earth-wall.
Thus was chase offered
to the Swedish nation
as Hygelac's boar-standard flew
and his troops overran the refuge place
where Hrethel's heirs

had thronged to garrison.

It was there

that the grizzle-haired Ongentheow

was brought to bay

and had to submit to Eofor's sole judgment:

Wulf Wonreding first struck

the old king with his sword

and made blood stream

from under his hair,

but the aged Scylfing was neither afraid

nor as yet in his death-sleep,

so with a deadlier stroke Ongentheow

sorely wounded Wulf

and brought him down

with a swift sword-stoke.

Eofor saw Wulf

bow down before the old king's sword

and with his broad blade and giant's helm

he broke over the shield-wall

and struck the Scylfing lord a fatal blow.

Many came to Wulf's aid,

and when room was cleared for them

in the war-field,

he was bandaged

and quickly raised up.

After that, they were able

to win the slaughter-place.

Then stripped one man the other's corpse.

They took from death-cold Ongentheow

his iron byrnie, his hard-hilted sword,

and his helmet, too.

And so it was
they carried the hoary king's armor
to Hygelac,
who claimed those treasured war-relics
and pledged fair rewards among his troops,
making good his promises of gifts to them.
When they reached their home-land,
the Geat-lord, Hrethel's heir,
paid for the war-clash as he had promised.
To Eofor and Wulf he gave much treasure.
He gave them both
a hundred-thousand worth of land
and linked rings;
no man on middle-earth
could reproach them such bounty
for they had gained many glories in war.
To Eofor, Hygelac also gave his only daughter,
Hygd, as favor's pledge.

This, then, is the source of the death-hate,
the feud and the enmity between our peoples,
for which I expect the Swedes to attack us
when they learn that our leader is gone from life,
he who formerly guarded his hoard and kingdom
against his enemies.
When Beowulf became king,
his keen shield-fighters upheld the folk
and gained much glory
when they dared great deeds
in his name.
Now, we must hasten to send

our tribe-king

and ring-giver on his pyre-journey.

We will melt no mere pittance

with our mighty lord

but a treasure-hoard of gold

uncounted and grimly purchased;

with his own life he has bought his last rings.

No man shall wear these treasures

in our king's memory,

no fair woman will wear on her neck

the ring-ornaments.

We will all be sad-hearted

and bereft of gold,

and not once but often

will we tread alien land

now that our

war-leader

has set aside laughter, pleasure,

and merriment

The flames will enfold him,

the blaze devour all.

Therefore will morning-cold spears

be raised in ever-fewer hands.

The harp-sway will not awaken our warriors,

but we will hear the black raven

eager for doomed flesh,

screeching to the eagle

how he fared at feasting

when he with the wolf despoiled the slain."

So, the messenger was bold

in the telling of hateful tidings;

he did not lie in deeds or words.

The troop all arose, sad-hearted,

and went to Earnaness

with welling tears to gaze at the wonder.

On the sand

they found their ring-giver

of former times

keeping his death-bed;

the end-day for the good man had come.

Their war-king, Wederas' chieftain,

had died in battle with a dragon,

a death

worthy of many songs and stories

and much praise.

Beside their chief lay his slayer,

the serpent.

The fire-dragon was fifty

foot-measures long

as it lay upon the sand,

gruesome and grim-hued,

scorched by flames.

This strange creature,

a loathsome beast,

had ruled the night with his flame-power

for a while,

then went back to seek his barrow,

secure in his earth-den

surrounded by cups and flagons,

plates and precious swords

eaten through by rust,

ruined as if they had stayed in earth's clasp

a thousand winters.

That hoard-legacy of past power

—former men's gold with spells surrounded—

was thrown open

and the people saw

that keeping the gold had not gained glory

for any who had hidden the treasure

under the wall.

The glorious chieftain

who had put the hoard in the barrow

had deeply cursed it,

defending it to the death

of him and all his kin.

Any who came after that

to plunder the place

would be made captive in a cage,

in death-bonds firm, tormented by woes.

It is a hard thing

to ponder where the courage-famed man

shall meet his fate

and end his destined life

when he may no longer inhabit his mead-hall

with his kin-folk.

So it was for Beowulf.

When he sought the barrow's guardian

and engaged him in fierce combats,

he did not know it would take him

from this world.

Wiglaf, son of Weohstan, spoke:

"Often, through the will of one man

many will suffer anguish

as has happened now to us.

We could not lend our loved chieftain

and kingdom-keeper any advice—

either to confront the gold-guard

or to let him lie where he long had,

occupying his haunts until the world's end—

Beowulf held firmly to his high destiny.

It was a harsh fate that drove our ruler

to go in under the stone wall

to hunt that barrow's guardian.

Then, after my king

un-gently cleared the way,

I went inside

and examined the room's treasures.

In haste I seized with my hands

a huge portion

from the vast burden of hoarded wealth

and brought it out to my lord.

He was still alive then, alert and aware,

able to enjoy

the sight of the barrow-wealth

for a little while.

The old man in his grief

said many things,

and told me to greet you

and tell you to build him a high mound,

a pyre spot

worthy of his friend-deeds.

We will build him a high barrow

great and glorious,

for he was the worthiest warrior

of all men through the wide earth.

Now let us hasten once more,

see and seek the heap of skill-gems,

the wonder under the wall.

I will guide you so that you also

can gaze upon the rings and broad gold.

Let the pyre be readied and quickly built.

When we come out,

we will then take our lord,

our loved man,

where he must long sleep

in Fate's keeping."

Then Wiglaf told the battle-brave heroes,

warriors, and dwelling-owners

to fetch the flame-wood from far and near

and bring it to the good man's presence.

He said,

"Now shall fire consume the warriors' ruler

and darken him with flame,

he who often braved

the iron-shower over the shield-wall,

the storm of feathered shafts

impelled by strings,

shot true

and eagerly following the iron heads."

The wise son of Weohstan

chose from the core of king-thanes

seven of the finest men

and went with them,

their eighth in number,

under the enemy roof.

One of them bore a torch in his hands

and walked in front.

No one drew lots

to see who would

plunder the useless hoard

that remained

on the ground in the barrow.

No one lamented

as they quickly carried out

the precious treasures.

They shoved the dragon over the sea-cliff

where the flood enfolded the jewels' keeper

and the waves carried him away.

Countless pieces of plated gold

in all shapes were laden

on a wagon with the king,

hoary battle-warrior,

and carried to Hronesness.

The Geats' people made ready

an unpaltry pyre on the earth

and hung it with helmets,

battle-shields, and bright byrnies,

as Beowulf had bade.

The heroes raised loud lament

when they laid in the midst of the treasure

their most beloved lord and famed chieftain.

Then the warriors began

to kindle the greatest of bale-fires

in the funeral mound.

Wood-smoke arose, black above the blaze.

Writhing flames wove with weeping

until the bone-house,

hot at heart, was broken.

Sorrow-minded and grief-laden,

they moaned their loved-lord's death

while a Geatish woman

with her hair bound up

sang a sorrowful death-dirge for Beowulf.

She sang anew

of torture and captivity

in the coming days,

of war and terror and much slaughter.

Heaven swallowed the smoke.

After ten days, the Wederas' people

covered the burnings' remains

with a shelter

built up on the headland,

high and broad,

widely visible for wave-farers.

Beowulf's beacon was encircled with a wall,

cleverly constructed by the worthiest of men.

Inside, they placed rings and brooches

and all such trappings

as men had removed

from the hoard.

They gave the gold back to the earth

to hold in its grit,

where it still stands,

as useless to men as it ever was.

Then around that barrow

rode twelve mounted battle-brave men,

sons of nobles

who wished to mourn their king,

lament their sorrow.

It is fitting that men honor their friend-lord

with words and heart-love

when he must give up his bone-house.

They made a song

which men still sing about Beowulf,

and in this manner did the Geats' people,

Beowulf's hearth-companions,

lament their lord's fall:

They praised

his courage-deeds and his heroic acts,

exalted his excellence.

They said of him

that of all the world-kings

he was the mildest and most gentle,

to his nation the kindest,

and a man most glad to win glory.